# THE MATTIS WAY OF WAR: AN EXAMINATION OF OPERATIONAL ART IN TASK FORCE 58 AND 1ST MARINE DIVISION

A thesis presented to the Faculty of the U.S. Army
Command and General Staff College in partial
fulfillment of the requirements for the
degree

# ABSTRACT

THE MATTIS WAY OF WAR: AN EXAMINATION OF OPERATIONAL ART IN TASK FORCE 58 AND 1ST MARINE DIVISION, by Major Michael L. Valenti, USMC, 98 pages.

This thesis examines the generalship, leadership, and operational art of General James N. Mattis, US Marine Corps by using Task Force 58 in Afghanistan as a formative base and then comparing elements of operational art to the conduct of the 1st Marine Division in Operation Iraqi Freedom, 2003. Mattis draws upon many historical influences that shape his operational design in both campaigns. He puts great effort and focus on ensuring that his commander's intent is understood by all his subordinates and uses a preference for a small staff in the planning and execution of his intent. He makes heavy use of personally selected liaison officers to form and sustain habitual relationships with higher and adjacent units. Through the use of historical examples and a refusal to be constrained by doctrine and popular thought he uses innovative approaches in his design. These innovative approaches often constitute paradigm shifts with contemporary thought and doctrine. A 'Mattis Way of War' is postulated in the conclusion which draws from his use of history, commander's intent, and leadership to build up a capacity, or potential energy, for action in his unit. Once built up, he unleashes this energy utilizing explicit trust in his staff and subordinates.

# ACKNOWLEDGMENTS

I wish to thank my wife, Colleen, for her unrelenting support in this endeavor. My long nights and weekends sequestered in the basement left her to care for our children and run the house. She never complained. To my children, Mickey and Brigid, thank you for being "good" during the "best year of our lives." I hope someday my example of hard work and dedication will become apparent to you. Thank you to my in-laws, Kevin and Susan for their frequent trips to Kansas to help my family and keep us sane.

Much appreciation and gratitude is felt for a variety of people at CGSC: my fellow Art of War Scholars for the invaluable feedback they have given me for this thesis; Dr. Dean Nowowiejski for having the confidence in me to finish this thesis, when I lacked the confidence myself; Col John Sullivan, USMC (Ret) for giving me the mentorship and motivation that only one Marine could give to another; and to my committee members for providing me with feedback and showing remarkable patience.

I wish to thank the United States Marine Corps History Division for aiding me in my research and providing me with a wealth of information, especially Mr. Tom Baughn. Mr. Vincent Goulding of the Marine Corps Warfighting Lab wrote an article in the *Marine Corps Gazette* that spurred my interest in Task Force 58. For all those I forgot to mention, thank you.

Within one hour of contacting General Mattis, he responded with a wealth of information and offers to assist me in this project. His material and the interview he honored me with have been invaluable. He is a true steward of our profession.

Finally, I wish to thank my father, Bill, and my mother, Angie, for all the support they have given me and the confidence they have bestowed upon me. My mother's unexpected death during this thesis dealt a hard blow from which I was not sure I could recover. I am confident that she has given me the strength to pick myself up, is watching over me, and excited to see me finish and return to my family. The streets to heaven are guarded by United States Marines and no doubt my brothers there embraced her when she entered. I love you. Semper Fidelis! Go Navy! Beat Army!

# TABLE OF CONTENTS

# ACRONYMS

ARG          Amphbious Ready Group

CENTCOM   US Central Command

CP            Command Post

DOD          Department of Defense

FOB          Forward Operating Base

ISB           Intermediate Staging Base

LOC          Logistics Operations Center

MAGTF       Marine Air Ground Task Force

MEB          Marine Expeditionary Brigade

MEF          Marine Expeditionary Force

MEU          Marine Expeditionary Unit

OIF           Operation Iraqi Freedom

# ILLUSTRATIONS

CHAPTER 1

INTRODUCTION

<u>Overview and Biography</u>

This thesis examines General James N. Mattis's staffing philosophies, the influence of history on his operational planning and execution, and his general command and leadership philosophies using Task Force 58 as a formative base. Then a brief look at his time commanding the 1st Marine Division in Operation Iraqi Freedom (OIF) examines whether his philosophies and concepts remained consistent or evolved. A chapter dedicated to his command philosophies and leadership explores common themes that were present during both periods and their influence on his later generalship.

General Mattis is an iconic figure in recent Marine Corps history and is known by many nicknames such as Mad Dog and the Warrior Monk. He gets the latter because of his intense love and study of military history, leadership, and the art of war. He had humble beginnings; born in a small town in the Pacific Northwest at the base of the Columbia River which had deep-rooted agricultural ties and a nuclear industry. His father was a Merchant Mariner and his mother worked with United States Army intelligence in South Africa. Growing up, his family never had a television, but had a rather extensive library. He has never married.[1]

After retiring in June of 2013, Mattis completed over forty-one years of service. He commanded at all levels including Recruiting Station Portland, 1st Battalion 7th Marines, 7th Marines (reinforced), 1st Marine Expeditionary Brigade, Task Force 58, 1st Marine Division, Marine Corps Combat Development Command, I Marine Expeditionary Force, US Joint Forces Command, and US Central Command.[2]

1

In response to the attacks of 9/11, the United States had to determine which military options in its arsenal would be best suited for the initial campaign in Afghanistan. There was initially much debate amongst President George W. Bush and his National Security Council as to the form of America's initial response. The debate focused between the use of the Central Intelligence Agency and the Department of Defense (DOD) to lead the military response. When asked what the military could provide in the way of developing the campaign, Secretary of Defense Donald Rumsfeld said "very little, effectively."[3]

Secretary Rumsfeld had to develop DOD options quickly and relied heavily on the input of two men: General Hugh Shelton, Chairman of the Joint Chiefs of Staff and General Tommy Franks, Commander of the US Central Command (CENTCOM). Rumsfeld's initial guidance was for "something creative between launching cruise missiles and an all-out military operation."[4] In order to meet the intent, General Franks quickly dismissed any Marine Corps option stating, "We can't make use of the Marines' amphibious capabilities. Whatever the final shape of the operation, it'll depend on airlift."[5] In his monograph entitled "U.S Marines in Afghanistan 2001-2002," Colonel Lowrey writes, "General Franks may have been acknowledging that the doctrinal capability of Marine expeditionary units limited amphibious operations to within 200 miles of the Pakistani coast."[6]

By September 14, 2001, the DOD had no options except for a cruise missile strike. General Franks summarized by stating, "The long poles of this operation will be access and sustainment. Any operation we conduct in Afghanistan will be dependent on airlift . . . thousands of tons a day."[7] Pressured to come up with courses of action the CENTCOM staff came up with the a four part plan: (1) Tomahawk missile strikes against Taliban and al-Qaeda forces in Afghanistan; (2) After the missile strike, conduct a three to ten day air war utilizing US Air Force bombers; (3) Following the missile and bomber attacks, put "boots on the ground" consisting of special operations forces from the Army, Navy, Air Force, and Central Intelligence Agency; and (4) Prosecute the first three options simultaneously then introduce conventional US Army and US Marine ground forces.[8]

Bush wanted something more than the military plan presented and initially dismissed the DOD's approach calling it "unimaginative."[9] On September 17, 2001, President Bush approved a separate Central Intelligence Agency option developed by Director George Tennant that involved a worldwide media plan and partnership with the Northern Alliance. He directed Secretary of State Colin Powell to issue an ultimatum to the Taliban "demanding that they turn over Osama bin Laden or suffer the consequences."[10] The consequences would take the form of the missile strikes and boots on the ground mentioned above. Rumsfeld was still pressuring the DOD to break the mold on conventional airlift stating, "This is chess, not checkers. We must be thinking beyond the first move."[11]

Units that could fulfill the boots on the ground requirement had to be mobilized and then transported to the theater of operations. Another option was to take already forward deployed units and retask them to support upcoming operations. Early in the planning process with focus on force protection and posturing already deployed units for a possible role in up and coming operations, General Franks ordered the Commander, 5th

Fleet and US Naval Forces Central Command to, "put [all ships] to sea and cancel future port visits to avoid the possibility of another incident like the bombing of the USS COLE."[12] This decision early on set the stage for Marines with the 15th Marine Expeditionary Unit MEU) currently in Darwin, Australia to put to sea and start focusing on other possible missions.

A MEU represents a powerful option to the president to project combat power. A MEU's organic aviation assets give it the capability to insert forces into an area with minimal outside assistance required. MEUs are trained to this standard and are already forward deployed. The two forward deployed MEUs with the capability to project combat power into Afghanistan were the 15th and 26th MEUs Special Operations Capable.[13] However, there was a significant challenge in projecting the Marines' combat power into Afghanistan. Forces would have to travel over 350 nautical miles inland to conduct operations. The use of aviation assets and Intermediate Staging Bases (ISBs) was the only feasible way to accomplish the mission. Before discussing employment of the MEUs and General Mattis's role, it is useful to explain several Marine doctrinal concepts and units.

<u>The Marine Air Ground Task Force</u>

The Marine Air Ground Task Force (MAGTF) is the principle fighting organization of the Marine Corps. It is a scalable (meaning that the size of the organization can be changed to suit its need) and tailorable organization consisting of four elements: Command Element, Ground Combat Element, Aviation Combat Element, and Logistics Combat Element. The MAGTF is commanded by a single commander who task organizes the formation in order to meet mission objectives which span the range of military operations.[14]

There are typically four types of MAGTFs based on size from largest to smallest are: Marine Expeditionary Force (MEF), Marine Expeditionary Brigades (MEB), MEU, and Special Purpose MAGTF (SPMAGTF). MAGTFs can best be identified by the size of the Ground Combat Element. A Marine division, regiment, and battalion constitute the Ground Combat Element for a MEF, MEB, and MEU respectively.[15] A SPMAGTF is a temporary MAGTF formed to conduct missions for which a MEF or other unit would not be appropriate or is not available (see figure 1).[16]

Photo Removed Due to Copyright Restrictions

Figure 1. MAGTF

*Source:* United States Marine Corps, "Marine Corps 101," October 17, 2013, accessed June 6, 2014, http://www.hqmc.marines.mil/Portals/61/MarineCorps101.pdf.

## The Marine Expeditionary Unit

The MEU is centered around a reinforced infantry battalion landing team which forms the Ground Combat Element. The Aviation Combat Element is composed of a composite squadron centered around a helicopter or tilt-rotor squadron with attached detachments from a Marine Attack Squadron (AV-8 Harrier), a Light Attack Squadron (UH-1Huey and AH-1Cobra), Heavy Helicopter Squadron (CH-53E Super Stallion), and an Aerial Refueler Transport Squadron (KC-130 Hercules). The Logistics Combat

Element is formed around a combat logistics battalion. The units are broken down and embarked on amphibious ships provided by the Navy. Together the MEU and the amphibious ships form an Amphibious Ready Group (ARG).[17]

The versatility of the MEU lies in its ability to project power, provide deterrence, and respond to a multitude of scenarios with organic assets. There are seven standing MEUs in the Marine Corps, three on each coast of the United States and one in the Pacific. They are designed to provide the nation with a continuous forward presence throughout the globe. The MEU is capable of fifteen days of sustainment while conducting operations ashore before needing to be resupplied.[18]

## Amphibious Operations

Assaults, raids, demonstrations, withdraws, and amphibious support to other operations comprise the five types of amphibious operations. Amphibious operations are conducted by amphibious forces consisting of an amphibious task force and a landing force. Amphibious operations are favorable to changing political situations because they generally do not require diplomatic clearances or host-nation support.[19]

Traditionally a beachhead is secured and is used to flow in follow on forces and build combat power. Amphibious operations tend to focus on littoral regions for this reason. With respect to Afghanistan and its land locked nature, an amphibious operation is still possible, but due to distances from sea ISBs were necessary to provide an area for buildup of forces and allow the refueling of aircraft.[20] The latter would prove to be a classic case of ship-to-objective maneuver.

## Formation of Task Force 58

Amphibious operations were initially dismissed for Afghanistan because of its landlocked nature as early as September 12, 2011. General Franks stated that amphibious operations were "untenable for Marine amphibious forces and that ground operations would require U.S. Army combat power supported by U.S. Air Force logistics."[21] This quick dismissal of a Marine component was based on the assumption that all forces would have to be flown in by the Air Force, and thus the ground component should be the Army. Marine Brigadier General John G. Castellaw, Deputy Commanding General, Marine Forces Pacific, quickly interjected and advocated for involvement of the Marine Corps. General Franks' dismissal of initial Marine involvement may have been due to an unfamiliarity of Marine Corps and Navy doctrine that had changed since the end of the cold war.[22]

The plan initially chosen by the president was to conduct a strategic bombing and missile strike campaign in Northern Afghanistan, striking targets that would "inform America's enemies that 'there is a dear price to be paid for actions like 9/11 that strike at the United States'."[23] However, the campaign did not effectively degrade the Taliban's capability and National Security Advisor Condoleezza Rice pointed out that a strategy and plan for countering the Taliban stronghold at Kandahar was needed.[24] The question stilled remained as to which units and by what means they would be utilized in the prosecution of the Taliban. A unit conducting an exercise in Egypt would ultimately answer that question.

Military deployments and operations were not completely halted after the events of 9/11. It was important to show the world that the United States was still committed to

8

its international partners by continuing to support previously negotiated operations. The United States had already committed to participate in a biannual training exercise with the Egyptians called Exercise Bright Star. The importance of this particular exercise was twofold: it served as a way to posture additional forces in the Middle East under the cover of an exercise and demonstrated America's resolve not to shy away from its commitments.[25] Brigadier General James N. Mattis wore many different hats during this period including: Commanding General of the 1st Marine Brigade (forces involved in Bright Star); Deputy Commanding General of I MEF; Commanding General, Marine Corps Forces, Central Command (Forward); and Combined Joint Task Force Consequence Management.[26]

Prior to his deployment for Exercise Bright Star, General Mattis had the foresight to prepare his Marines for possible action in response to the terrorist attacks. His foresight coupled with the determination of General Castellaw to get the Marines in the fight eventually led to the formation of Task Force 58. General Castellaw advocated the idea of a composite amphibious brigade for use by CENTCOM for operations in Afghanistan. After one of the capstone exercises in Bright Star, this plan came to fruition and Task Force 58 was born. It was eventually to consist of two ARGs, the Bataan and Peleliu and use the headquarters of Bright Star for the command element (see figures 2, 3, and 4).[27] The 13th MEU appears in figure 4 because it eventually relieved the 15th MEU. For the purposes of this thesis, the actions of the 13th MEU will not be considered or included because they did not participate in the initial formation of the task force or seizure of FOB Rhino.

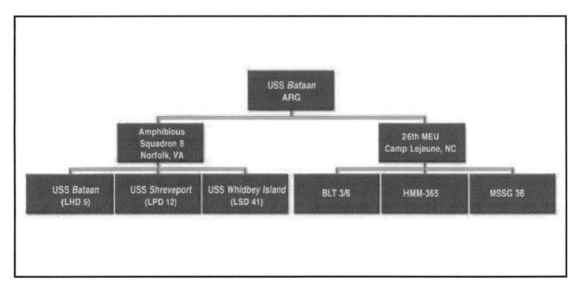

Figure 2.   USS *Bataan* ARG

*Source:* Nathan S. Lowrey, *U.S. Marines In Afghanistan, 2001-2002: FROM THE SEA: U.S. Marines in the Global War on Terrorism* (Washington, DC: United States Marine Corps History Division, 2011), 72.

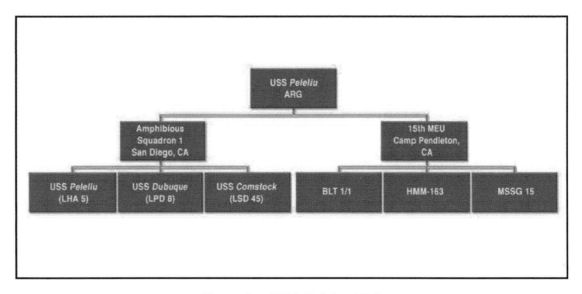

Figure 3.   USS *Peleliu* ARG

*Source:* Nathan S. Lowrey, *U.S. Marines In Afghanistan, 2001-2002: FROM THE SEA: U.S. Marines in the Global War on Terrorism* (Washington, DC: United States Marine Corps History Division, 2011), 23.

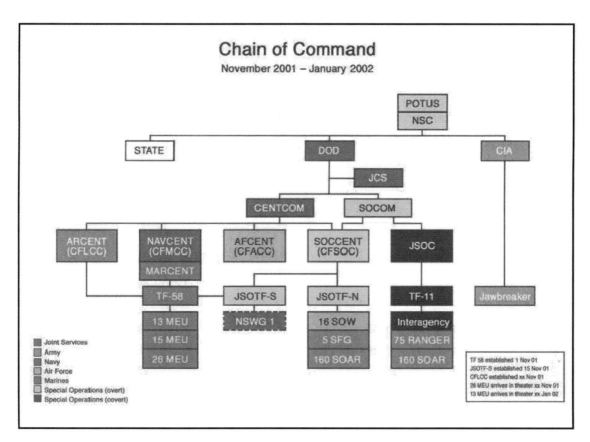

Figure 4.   Chain of Command

*Source:* Nathan S. Lowrey, *U.S. Marines In Afghanistan, 2001-2002: FROM THE SEA: U.S. Marines in the Global War on Terrorism* (Washington, DC: United States Marine Corps History Division, 2011), 91.

Primary Research Question

Using Task Force 58 as a formative base, how did General Mattis's theories on historical influences, staff organization, and leadership influence the planning and conduct of Task Force 58's operations, and how did they evolve or remain constant during his command of the 1st Marine Division in OIF in 2003?

## Secondary Research Questions

Did his innovations work? Are they worthy of repeating?

Did his style evolve as he increased in responsibility?

What role did current doctrine play in the planning and execution of the Task Force 58's mission?

Were exceptions to doctrine necessary to accomplish the mission?

What specific shortfalls existed in leadership/command and control, task organization, and planning that proved to be hindrances to mission accomplishment?

## Assumptions

All Marine Corps units participating in Task Force 58 were trained and equipped to accomplish their original missions as part of the MEU.

Upon their original deployment as part of separate MEU's, there was no anticipation of combining the forces.

The reader is familiar with the general events surrounding Task Force 58 and the 1st Marine Division in OIF I.

## Scope and Delimitations

This study is intended to look critically at General Mattis's staffing philosophy, how history influenced his concepts, and his philosophy of leadership and command. It is not meant to be an authoritative examination of Task Force 58 or the 1st Marine Division's role in OIF circa 2003.

The thesis will only analyze Task Force 58 from the time immediately following 9/11 through February 26, 2002, and not analyze the Marine Corps' involvement in

Operation Anaconda. Similarly, the thesis will only examine the period from General

Mattis's assumption of command of the 1st Marine Division through the end of the

opening events in the invasion of Iraq.

---

[1] Gen James N. Mattis, interview by Harry Kreisler, March 20, 2014, interview #28135, Conversations with History, University of California at Berkley, Berkley, CA, University of California Television, accessed August 29, 2014, http://www.uctv.tv/ shows/Reflections-with-General-James-Mattis-Conversations-with-History-28135. Referred to hereafter as Mattis-Kreisler interview.

[2] Headquarters, United States Marine Corps, "Official Biography: General James N. Mattis," accessed November 8, 2014, https://slsp.manpower.usmc.mil/gosa/ biographies/rptBiography.asp?PERSON_ID=121&PERSON_TYPE=General.

[3] Nathan S. Lowrey, *U.S. Marines In Afghanistan, 2001-2002: FROM THE SEA: U.S. Marines in the Global War on Terrorism* (Washington, DC: United States Marine Corps History Division, 2011), 21.

[4] Ibid., 23.

[5] Ibid., 24.

[6] Ibid.

[7] Ibid., 25.

[8] Ibid.

[9] Ibid.

[10] Ibid., 26.

[11] Ibid.

[12] Ibid., 21.

[13] Commander, Task Force 58, "Task Force 58 Command Chronology for the Period 27 October to 26 February 2002," February 21, 2002, 7-8. Referred to hereafter as "Task Force 58 Command Chronology."

[14] United States Marine Corps, Marine Corps Doctrinal Publication (MCDP) 1-0, *Marine Corps Operations* (Washington, DC: Headquarters, United States Marine Corps, 2011), 2-6.

[15] Ibid., 2-9.

[16] Ibid., 3-19.

[17] Ibid., 2-12 - 2-13.

[18] Ibid., 2-13 – 2-14.

[19] Chairmen Joint Chiefs of Staff, Joint Publication (JP) 3-02, *Amphibious Operations* (Washington, DC: US Government Printing Office, 2014), I-2.

[20] "Task Force 58 Command Chronology," 10.

[21] Lowrey, 34.

[22] Ibid.

[23] Ibid., 51.

[24] Ibid., 56.

[25] Ibid., 66.

[26] Ibid., 70.

[27] Ibid., 70-73.

CHAPTER 2

TASK FORCE 58

Overview

This chapter will examine the formation and structure of General Mattis's staff. A discussion on doctrinal influences on the command and control of Task Force 58 will demonstrate where a departure in doctrine was needed in order to effectively employ the units in the operation. A case study detailing the seizure of Forward Operating Base (FOB) Rhino will illustrate the staff process. Finally, historical influences are analyzed that contributed to the operational design of the operation and its execution.

General Mattis's Staff in Task Force 58

Simply put, the problem General Mattis had to solve was how to project combat power ashore in order to disrupt Taliban command and control in Southern Afghanistan.[1] An inject into the enemy system was needed in order to deny him freedom of action. Mattis was aware of this and told his staff "Okay, this is what we're going to do. We're going to get over there and form a very small team [staff] . . . and we're going to start thinking about what we are going to do to go kick some ass."[2] The notion of a small staff was born both out of necessity, lack of physical space, and personal style. Efficiencies gained from a small staff generate speed in orders production and execution that proved to be instrumental in the accomplishment of his mission. Before that speed could be realized, General Mattis had to shed some responsibilities and trim the staff.

Mattis wore many different hats and was charged with a myriad of responsibilities. He was Commanding General of the 1st Marine Brigade; Deputy

Commanding General for I MEF; Commanding General for Marine Corps Forces, Central Command (Forward); and Commanding General for Combined Joint Task Force Consequence Management.[3] Until he was relieved of some of these responsibilities, General Mattis had to accomplish multiple missions with a staff that was designed for the planning and execution of Bright Star. On October 29th, Mattis was gradually relieved of his additional duties so that he could focus on operations in Afghanistan.[4] As of October 31st, his staff consisted of six personnel: three Marines from 1st MEB, two Marines from Marine Corps Forces Central Command, and a single Marine from Task Force Consequence Management.[5]

Once free to concentrate his efforts exclusively on operations in Afghanistan, his staff and command structure started to take shape. US Navy Vice Admiral Charles W. Moore, commander of US Naval Forces Central Command and Combined Forces Maritime Component Commander, designated General Mattis as commander of Naval Expeditionary Task Force 58. This designation flew in the face of current doctrine that called for a naval officer to command an amphibious task force.[6] Admiral Moore's rationalization was simple and profound. In the doctrine of amphibious operations, the commander of the amphibious force and commander of the landing force participated in a supporting and supported relationship. Admiral Moore surmised that because there was no coastal threat, and significant coordination between ground combat operations, Special Operations Forces, and the Northern Alliance would be necessary, the amphibious force commander would be in a supporting relationship to the landing force commander. By putting Mattis in charge of the Naval Expeditionary Task Force, Admiral Moore generated significant operational flexibility and authority for him.[7]

16

Two key constraints played a significant role in the necessity of a small staff: the limited space available in Bahrain and the lack of an amphibious command ship.[8] Mattis eventually settled on a staff of approximately thirty-two individuals. He used a concept that he coined "Skip Echelon."[9] Essentially Skip Echelon eliminated redundancy at various levels of the command. For example, not every level necessitated a chaplain, public affairs officer, medical personnel, etc. If these personnel were required to perform a function, they would simply Skip Echelon up or down the chain of command in order to fulfill their requirement.

Mattis's concept of Skip Echelon may have been influenced by British Field Marshal Sir William Joseph Slim. Slim asserts that there are three ways to cut down staffs: a flat cut (reduction by ten percent for example), cut out one complete tier of staff hierarchy, or eliminate complete sections.[10] In Mattis's, mind the elimination of complete sections could work as long as the flow of information within the staff was open and its members were willing to working together.[11] Mattis employed Skip Echelon by eliminating the surgeon, staff judge advocate, chaplain, and sergeant major from his staff. If these staff functions were needed, he would use them from subordinate units.[12]

Upon further research, it was discovered that General Mattis's use of Skip Echelon was influenced by a major in the Iraqi Army that his battalion took prisoner in the Gulf War. Through interrogation, the prisoner revealed that Skip Echelon was a practice in the Iraqi Army.[13] At one time, Iraq was a colony of Britain, so Slim's influence could have still been relevant.

Mattis gave guidance on the construction of his staff. He wanted "a small staff comprised of aggressive officers who were able to act with initiative, make rapid decisions and recommendations, and exercise good judgment."[14] Due to the small size of

the staff and few enlisted Marines to support it, General Mattis made it clear that

everyone had to "fill sandbags."[15] The initial tempo of planning was intense and as new

members arrived to fill positions, they had to be caught up to speed quickly and get right

to work. In order to expedite this process the creation of a "Brain Book" was

implemented. The book consisted of various references and orders that were needed to

get new members up to speed quickly. The Brain Book by itself would not be enough, the

professionalism, willingness, and doctrinal foundation of the new members of the staff

would carry them the rest of the way.[16]

General Mattis's personal feelings about staff size are worthy of comment and

discussion. He believed that a smaller staff would have more shared situational awareness

and be faster in reacting to changes in situations and opportunities presented by the

enemy.[17] These qualities would be important in the environment in which Task Force 58

was going to fight. The distances that had to be traveled to reach objectives were

enormous and unforgiving. A large staff tends to take on a bureaucratic nature and can

oppose the speed of planning and information sharing. Elements of operations, plans for

support, and intricacies of details could not afford to be lost or misunderstood. He

believed that if his staff had more of a human face rather than a large mass of people, the

bureaucratic process would decrease and be less procedurally driven thus increasing

speed.[18]

In the formation of the staff, Mattis gave less concern to finding the perfect staff

officer in order to build the perfect staff. It was believed that each individual possessed

certain capabilities that when employed in concert with other individuals with different

18

and complimentary capabilities would create a synergy where the sum of the parts is greater than the whole. This synergistic effect was accepted and staff members were encouraged to think critically beyond typical solutions to problems and come up with solutions that creatively used resources to solve problems. The capability of an individual meant most, sometimes even more than rank. Egos did not have a place at the table and were quickly tamed.[19]

General Mattis is a huge proponent of the book *Good to Great* by Jim Collins.[20] In this book, Collins focuses initially on getting the right people on board in your organization and getting the wrong people out.[21] There was a natural selection process in the staff of Task Force 58, where only the strong survived. Mattis marginalized the weak and the other members of the staff and their duties and responsibilities were absorbed by more competent members of the staff. Cut out of the circle of trust, the weaker members who failed to step up were eventually sent back to their parent commands.[22]

Now that his core staff was formed and focused on planning initial operations into Southern Afghanistan, General Mattis had to construct a command climate that fostered interoperability between the 15th and 26th MEUs and the Navy ships they were aboard. In order to ease confusion and enable a tighter integration of the Navy and Marine Corps team, General Mattis adopted the "N" section nomenclature used by the Navy vice the "G" and "S" designations used by the Marine Corps.[23] For example, his logistics section would be the N4 shop vice the G4 shop. He originally just wanted to have a plans section (N5) only and did not see the need for an operations section (N3). The insatiable thirst for information from higher proved this impossible and he later created an N3 operations section.[24]

<u>MEU Relationships</u>

The Task Force 58 staff needed to integrate its efforts with the two MEU staffs. Three independent staffs existed in Task Force 58: the Headquarters Staff (Task Force 58 staff), the 15th MEU staff, and the 26th MEU staff. Integration and unity of effort between the staffs would be pivotal in the success of any operation.

One option considered, but disregarded was; to integrating MEU staff efforts would be to combine the two MEUs into a MEB. This would enable Task Force 58 to have a single commander for each part of the MAGTF. The Command Element would be the Task Force 58 headquarters under Mattis. The two separate Aviation Combat Elements, Logistics Combat Elements, and Ground Combat Elements would be combined and their new commanders selected from within the existing MEU construct. However, within the current time constraints these new command relationships would be difficult to form and exercise. Adding to the friction, communications between the combined seven Navy ships would also be difficult. Had the MEB been formed prior to deployment and been given the chance to train and operate as such, command and control and relationships could have been developed and honed.

Another reason why the combining of the two MEUs would not be advantageous is that the MEU is set up to be very independent. Each MEU trains together for deployment and institutes multiple Special Operating Procedures that curtail planning time and aid to standardize multiple complex mission sets. Combining two MEUs under these circumstances would have been possible, but it would have hindered their ability to use each of their own common training bases to rapidly and safely execute complex missions.

Another consideration was that initial missions for Task Force 58 were a series of raids of undetermined length.[25] There was no perceived need for a massed land force of two Battalion Landing Teams that constituted the Ground Combat Element of each MEU. A method that maximizes the previous training and cohesiveness requisite in each MEU and provides for maximum operational flexibility was needed. Keeping the MEUs separate and establishing a supporting and supported relationship depending on the mission was the most logical choice under the circumstances. Had the two MEUs combined to form a MEB, the resultant Ground Combat Element would have been a Regimental Landing Team minus. The commander of this new unit would most likely have been the senior battalion commander. He would now have to control a unit that had not trained together and spend precious time forming his own staff and merging the two separate units. Given the already complex and time sensitive nature of the operation, this would have been a recipe for disaster.

## Doctrinal Influences

It is useful to look at the influence of doctrine (or lack of understanding) on the decision to include or exclude Marine Corps forces as a viable option to conduct operations early on in what would become Operation Enduring Freedom. On September 12, 2001, General Franks, commander in chief of CENTCOM, began to develop military options for the president and joint chiefs. The early dismissal of Marine Corps capabilities by General Franks was indicative of the lack of understanding of post-Cold War amphibious doctrine.[26] Cold War amphibious doctrine was largely centered on countering the Soviet global maritime threat.[27] At the time of the 9/11 attacks the advertised Marine amphibious capability was the insertion of a battalion overland or by

21

air to an objective 200 nautical miles away.[28] The landlocked nature of Afghanistan coupled with limited strategic access may have caused the oversight of Marine capabilities by senior leadership.

Contemporary Marine Corps doctrine compares the capabilities of an expeditionary force with that of a traditional land force in Marine Corps Doctrinal Publication 3, *Expeditionary Operations*: "In general, naval expeditionary forces provide a self-sustaining, sea-based capability for immediate or rapid response, especially through forward deployment. Land-based forces, on the other hand, generally require a longer deployment phase and the creation of an in-theater logistics apparatus to achieve the buildup of decisive force."[29] Applying this difference in forces to the situation after the terrorist attacks, it is apparent that an expeditionary force would be most suited as the initial conventional force to execute combat operations in Afghanistan. The organic aviation assets of the MEU further its capability to deploy its sea-based force utilizing ship to objective maneuver rather than ship to shore movement.

Doctrine was of little utility when it came time to frame the command and control network of the newly created expeditionary force. Contemporary doctrine called for a Commander Landing Force and a Commander Amphibious Task Force that shared a supported and supporting relationship. Generally the Commander Landing Force would be assumed by the Marine Corps (if a Marine unit was the landing force) and the Commander Amphibious Task Force would be assumed by the Navy.[30] In a break from doctrine, a Marine general (Mattis) was put in command of all amphibious forces and shipping. This was unprecedented for the time, but simplified the command relationships within the task force. Mattis would keep his staff small and create broad operational

22

concepts while the MEU commander executing the operation would fill in the details, and the other MEU assumed a supporting role.[31]

## Task Force 58 Staff Process: A Case Study—Rhino

The general planning construct for the Task Force 58 staff and the two MEUs was simple in theory. The Task Force 58 staff concentrated on operational planning, developing plans, validating targets, and providing mission type orders to the MEU that was going to execute the mission.[32] The Task Force 58 staff handed off the concept plan to the executing MEU and then started planning the next mission. The non-executing MEU would have a supporting relationship to the executing MEU. This supporting and supported method provided the MEU commanders with the widest possible latitude in the successful execution of the mission.[33] The individual MEUs were able to capitalize on their previous training and standard operating procedures to accomplish their missions without wasting time trying to form new units.

In order to comply with Admiral Moore's original intent of conducting raids, three courses of action were developed: first, a six- to twelve-hour company sized short duration raid; second a twenty-four- to thirty-six-hour near simultaneous raid employing two companies on two different objectives; and third, a forty-eight- to seventy-two-hour long duration raid consisting of a Battalion Landing Team.[34] Continual refinement of the plan, new intelligence information, and the realization of the need to seize a FOB in Southern Afghanistan led to a final mission of "seizing a FOB in order to attack lines of communications leading into Kandahar."[35]

In order to overcome the distance associated with operating in excess of 350 nautical miles inland, ISBs were necessary to provide for refueling of aviation assets, forward staging of personnel and equipment, and shorten the logistical chain. Close

coordination with the American Embassy in Islamabad, Pakistan, Marine liaison officers,

and CENTCOM yielded three ISBs in Pakistan: Pasni, Shamsi, and Jacobabad (see figure

5).[36]

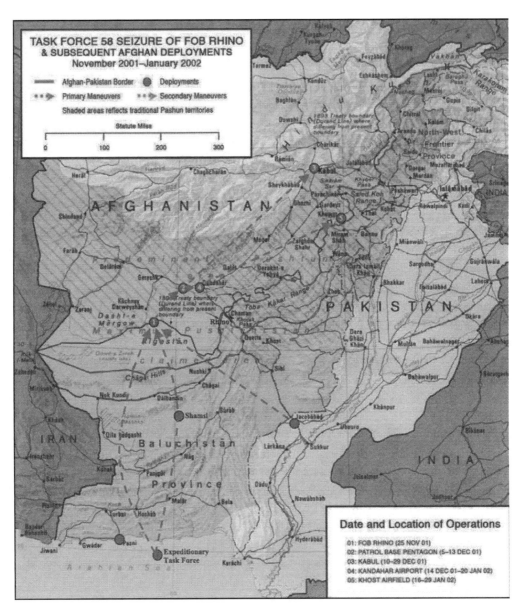

Figure 5.   FOB Rhino and ISBs

*Source:* Nathan S. Lowrey, *U.S. Marines In Afghanistan, 2001-2002: FROM THE SEA: U.S. Marines in the Global War on Terrorism* (Washington, DC: United States Marine Corps History Division, 2011), 112.

General Mattis purposefully kept the Task Force 58 staff looking forward in time and anticipating requirements. They were able to do this because they did not have to get involved with the details of the two MEUs. This paid off on November 10, 2001, during a concept of operations brief the staff was giving to the Deputy Commander in Chief of CENTCOM when they were instructed to continue planning for operations in Southern Afghanistan and start preparing for seizing and holding a FOB.[37] The staff was already looking at Rhino that was a hunting camp complete with a 6,400-foot dirt runway and a couple of buildings. Rhino had been previously seized by 3d Battalion, 75 Ranger Regiment (Task Force 3/75) in support of Task Force Sword on October 17, 2001, then subsequently abandoned due to other mission requirements.[38]

As with any operational planning, friction plays an integral part that tends to cause a staff to plan and plan again due to changing situations. The objective changed from Kandahar Airport, to Heart, to Shindand, and finally back to Rhino.[39] Communication between the Task Force 58 staff and the MEU staffs was paramount in order to ease the frustration and obtain a unity of effort. In order to solidify and endorse the relationships within Task Force 58, General Mattis released a message addressed to the MEU and Amphibious Squadron commanders detailing that his top priority was to develop "a mutually supportive relationship between the two MEU commanders themselves."[40]

A MEU is designed to be a highly effective and self-contained organization able to execute missions independently utilizing their common training and standard operating procedures. The Task Force 58 staff looked to capitalize on that by assigning each MEU missions that would exploit their training and cohesiveness. The 15th MEU was tasked with seizing and securing FOB Rhino, and the 26th MEU was tasked with conducting the raid, interdiction, and seizure missions from Rhino.[41] The 15th MEU was specifically chosen for the seizure of Rhino because it had earlier planned to conduct operations at Rhino in support of Task Force Sword (a special operations unit conducting missions in Afghanistan). Due to a helicopter crash from a unit supporting Task Force Sword, the 15th MEU did not execute that mission. Instead, they executed missions to recover the downed aircraft from an airfield in Pakistan.[42]

The staff identified resource shortfalls and promulgated requests for forces. They ascertained that aviation assets from both MEUs were needed in the initial seizure of Rhino. This meant that roles and responsibilities for each MEU had to be clearly articulated and increased communication both laterally and up the chain of command was required and fostered. Throughout this process, the Task Force 58 staff outgrew their temporary accommodations at Naval Support Activity Bahrain and had to procure a new site in a parking lot. This was significant because their original spaces were never suited for a staff to occupy them. Navy SEABEES responded to the task and in record time constructed concrete pads and emplaced tents for the staff. The administrative friction with moving their headquarters in the middle of planning cannot be overstated. New email accounts were necessary and were created and disseminated. Every manner of logistical office supply from desks, pens, and paper to phones and printers had to be "acquired" in true Marine Corps fashion.[43]

It is important to note that at this time while the main staff for Task Force 58 was working out of makeshift accommodations in Bahrain, the other two MEUs were out conducting other missions. The 15th MEU was conducting security operations in

Jacobabad and awaiting relief from this tasking from the Army. The 26th MEU was

enroute to the area of operations and uncertain of their arrival time. Communication was

made possible via email and Video Teleconference. The different staffs had to coordinate

their planning efforts and were sometimes the last to know when plans were changed by

higher headquarters in Tampa.[44]

On November 20, 2001, nineteen members from the Task Force 58 staff at

Bahrain transitioned to the *Peleliu i*n preparation for the assault.[45] While this was not

easy, it was made easier by having a small staff. Billeting and working spaces on the

*Peleliu* were at a premium and as alluded to previously by Admiral Moore and General

Mattis, could not handle a large staff.

Once on board the *Peleliu*, the 15th MEU staff presented a three and a half hour

long formal confirmation brief for the seizure of FOB Rhino to General Mattis and his

staff. D-Day was set at 1700Z on November 23, 2001. It was an extremely detailed plan

and the "most complex landing plan in anyone's memory."[46] More detail was needed for

the flow of Marines to the ISBs in Pakistan and coordination was made with Marine

liaison elements in Pakistan. As a fitting end to the arduous days leading up to and

including the confirmation brief, a Thanksgiving Day meal was served on board the

ships. In order to reinforce lateral communication between the MEUs, liaisons were

crossdecked, or transferred, between ships in order to "reinforce the integrated nature of

[Task Force 58] and to continue coordination planning between the three staffs."[47]

Trust in his staff's capabilities allowed General Mattis to focus on commander

issues. One such instance was when he was reviewing the rules of engagement for the

assault force. He found them to be too restrictive because they required a hostile act or intent to be committed or demonstrated prior to the engagement of potential targets. He officially requested that all personnel in the landing zone be declared hostile which would allow the ground force commander to engage targets at will. This was initially met with resistance from the CENTCOM staff in Tampa, Florida. Naval Forces Central Command commander, Admiral Moore, probably because of his close relationship with General Mattis, fully supported the change citing that "our Marines required the freedom to proactively engage the enemy using their initiative and trusting the Marine's good judgment."[48] The request was later approved by CENTCOM.

D-Day was postponed until November 25th due to CENTCOM not issuing an execute order although the Marines were ready on the 23rd. Essentially the seizure of Rhino went off without any major complications. Colonel Thomas D. Waldhauser, Commanding Officer of the 15th MEU (Special Operations Capable), later recalled, "It was really . . . awesome . . . one of those days where things go well and you just have to savor it."[49]

On D+1, a Marine KC-130 flew in a forward observation post to Rhino consisting of General Mattis, a communications team, and a SEABEE liaison officer.[50] This observation post would serve as General Mattis's forward command post and stretched the Task Force 58 staff between three locations: Rhino, the USS *Peleliu*, and Bahrain.[51] Since he was now forward and technically still in command of the entire ARG, General Mattis designated Commodore William Jezierski (Commander, Amphibious Squadron One) as the Deputy Commander of Task Force 58. Prior to this designation, Mattis retained a chief of staff, but had not officially designated a deputy commander of Task Force 58 prior to November 28th.[52] The new designation facilitated the operational

28

control and tactical direction of the shipping assigned to Task Force 58 by allowing a senior naval officer to command both ARGs while Mattis was ashore. Commodore Jezierski was never caught flat-footed and was pivotal in the execution of what was believed to be the "most difficult amphibious landing in 20 years."[53]

Task Force 58's staff was effective by emphasizing close and detailed coordination through command relationships and liaison officers. The Task Force 58 staff was able to plan broad operational muscle movements and left the detailed planning to the respective MEUs. When the MEUs had to combine resources such as aviation assets for the initial assault into Rhino, the command climate established by General Mattis enabled them to do so via the heavy emphasis he placed on communication and liaison officers. The small Task Force 58 staff proved invaluable during this operation. It did not overwhelm the already crowded spaces on board the *Peleliu* and ensured that information flowed freely and timely throughout the operation and was not caught up in staff bureaucracy that can sometimes be inherent to larger staffs.

## Historical Influences

General Mattis is a huge advocate of the study of military history, and it was apparent in his operational approach to the conduct of operations in Task Force 58. General Mattis refers to using history as a guide to "practice informed boldness."[54] He advocates the use of history to "broaden your operational reach, giving you mental models that you can apply imaginatively."[55] He cites a number of historical examples that influenced his Task Force 58 operational design to include Major General Orde Charles Wingate's operations in Burma.[56] Other historical influences on the operational design include the firebase concept used during Vietnam and Grierson's Raids during the Civil

War.[57] As long as the historical context is understood, past operations can be used as a point of departure for the design of current operations. By examining the premise of Wingate's second raid into Burma, similarities can be drawn from the seizure of FOB Rhino and subsequent operations of Task Force 58.

In 1944, while operating in Burma under Field Marshal William Joseph Slim, Wingate devised a plan to infiltrate well behind Japanese lines by flying in his forces to rapidly transport his combat forces. His aim was that "a force, which penetrating behind the enemy lines, [could] operate in comparatively small, lightly-equipped columns to harry [the enemy's] communications and rear establishments."[58] When put next to Task Force 58's initial guidance of conducting raids in Southern Afghanistan and Mattis's summation of, "Give me 1,000 men ashore for 30 days and we could make the enemy's life hell on earth for raids"[59] the linkage becomes apparent. To solidify the linkage even more, one of Slim's objectives for Wingate was to "[inflict] the greatest possible damage and confusion on the enemy in North Burma."[60]

An interesting similarity between Wingate's forces and Mattis's is that Wingate was in command of a MAGTF-like unit (minus Marines of course). Wingate had under his command or at his direct disposal the No. 1 Air Commando (Aviation Combat Element), a Logistical Combat Element, and a Ground Combat Element. Using all three in concert, Wingate planned to fly his forces into Burma well behind enemy lines. Gliders flew in initial waves putting engineers in place to make open fields into improvised landing strips capable of accepting Dakota transport aircraft to facilitate a rapid build-up of combat power and logistical supplies.[61] This was much akin to the seizure of Rhino and subsequent efforts by SEABEES to get Rhino capable of accepting the venerable

Marine KC-130 combat transports. Wingate's operations in Burma served as a mental model, a point of departure for Mattis.

General Mattis also used Grierson's Raids in Mississippi during the American Civil War as a model demonstrating how a relatively small unit can cause chaos in the enemy's rear by attacking lines of communication.[62] A 1904 *U.S. Cavalry Association Journal* describes Grierson's raid as "a diversion in the rear, to assist Grant in his operations against Vicksburg, as well as to divide the 'Confederacy' and cut communication between [Vicksburg and Tennessee]."[63] Grierson's Raid put the enemy in a dilemma by making him choose to divert forces to counter the raid (thus taking some pressure off Grant) or to continue to have his lines of communications threatened. A similar dilemma for the enemy is found in one of the endstates in Mattis's commander's intent for Task Force 58 (emphasis is his): "Taliban/Al Qaida Leaders in disarray, facing an operational dilemma on how to allocate their forces (northern front or southern Afghanistan)."[64] Mattis further explains in his commander's intent (emphasis is his) that the raids were designed to "destroy the enemy's sense of security and shatter his will."[65] Grierson's Raid influenced Mattis's intent by giving him a mental model of what raid forces were capable of when inserted deep in the enemy's rear.

Mattis was able to make an adaptation on the firebase concept employed in Vietnam for use at FOB Rhino. A firebase was a temporary operating based composed of infantry and artillery from which the units could launch offensive actions.[66] He traded out artillery for aviation delivered fires that enabled him to bring more assault forces into FOB Rhino in the initial waves. Because of his established relationship with the Combined Forces Air Component Commander, General T. Michael Moseley, he was

31

confident that aviation delivered fires would be there if he needed them. General Moseley told Mattis that "if you get in any trouble, you just call [your LNOs], and I'll turn every airframe in the air over your head."[67] It was because of this relationship and trust that General Mattis left behind his artillery for the first time in thirty years.[68] General Mattis was able to adapt the firebase concept to fit his operational design in Afghanistan.[69]

## Conclusion

A small Task Force 58 staff proved to be less bureaucratic and eased the rapid and accurate flow of information. By using the technique of Skip Echelon, Mattis was able to keep functionality in his staff with fewer numbers. He stated, "keep the staff small unless you need constant, mindless reassurance."[70] A small staff worked for Mattis in this case because his subordinate MEU staffs were fully formed and staffed. This allowed him to utilize their staff functions that were not resident in his own staff. A key point, Mattis's small staff concept works only when subordinate units are entrusted with a wide degree of latitude in their planning and execution, and they possess the manpower and resources to plan effectively.

It is important to note that a small staff will not work in all situations such as when there is a need to communicate laterally with like units. For example, if one regiment in a division incorporated a small staff and Skip Echelon and the other regiments did not; lateral communication would be more difficult. In this situation there were no other like units involved. In order to facilitate communication with non-like units, Mattis used liaison officers extensively. Of his liaison officers he said, "LNO's are critical, you should always send someone you hate to lose."[71]

In the area of doctrine, one must be able to take doctrine as a starting point, but not the final answer. Doctrine should never constrain thinking or make the possible seemingly impossible. Mattis wrote, "Combat experience or confined thinking in doctrinally constrained exercises can be as much a mental straitjacket as a lack of such experience, unless broadened by historical study and happy hour conversations [or] challenges."[72] Had normal staff doctrine been employed as written, Task Force 58 would have faced numerous command and control problems. In fact, operational doctrine might have led to a unit like Task Force 58 never being considered to perform an amphibious assault over 200 nautical miles inland.

Finally, the use of historical examples as mental models can serve as a point of departure for innovations. History will not repeat itself, but as long as the context is understood, it can lay the cognitive framework for innovative solutions to complex problems. General Mattis's appreciation for and understanding of historical examples laid the framework for the ground breaking tactical employments of his task force.

---

[1] Lowrey, 80.

[2] Ibid., 67.

[3] Ibid., 70.

[4] Ibid., 79.

[5] Ibid., 80.

[6] Chairman Joint Chiefs of Staff, JP 3-02, xii.

[7] Lowrey, 80.

[8] Ibid., 82.

[9] Commander, Task Force 58, "Thoughts About TF58: Nov 2001-Apr 2002," November 23, 2010. Referred to hereafter as "Task Force 58 Thoughts."

[10] Field Marshal Sir William Slim, "Kermit Roosevelt Lecture" (lecture, US Army Command and General Staff College, Fort Leavenworth, KS, April 8, 1952).

[11] Gen James N. Mattis, interview by Dr. Gary Solis, June 18, 2007, interview 0052, transcript, Marine Corps Oral History Program, Marine Corps History and Museum Division, Quantico, VA, 5. Referred to hereafter Mattis-Solis interview.

[12] MajGen James N. Mattis, interview by Captain Crossland, February 24, 2002, interview CDR-699, transcript, Marine Corps Oral History Program, Marine Corps History and Museum Division, Quantico, VA, 9.

[13] Gen James N. Mattis, telephone interview with author, Lansing, KS, October 28, 2014. Referred to hereafter as Mattis-Valenti interview.

[14] "Task Force 58 Command Chronology," 10.

[15] Ibid., 11.

[16] Ibid., 12.

[17] Mattis-Solis interview, 3-4.

[18] Ibid.

[19] Lowrey, 85.

[20] Mattis-Solis interview, 7.

[21] James C. Collins, *Good to Great: Why Some Companies Make the Leap--and Others Don't* (New York: Harper Business, 2001), 63.

[22] Lowrey, 85.

[23] "Task Force 58 Command Chronology," 11.

[24] Ibid.

[25] Ibid., 12.

[26] Lowrey, 34.

[27] Ibid., 35.

[28] Ibid., 37.

[29] United States Marine Corps, Marine Corps Doctrinal Publication (MCDP) 3, *Expeditionary Operations* (Washington, DC: Headquarters, United States Marine Corps, 1998), 36.

[30] Lowrey, 81.

[31] "Task Force 58 Command Chronology," 9-14.

[32] Ibid., 13.

[33] Lowrey, 81.

[34] "Task Force 58 Command Chronology," 19.

[35] Ibid., 20.

[36] Ibid., 21.

[37] Ibid., 22.

[38] Lowrey, 59.

[39] "Task Force 58 Command Chronology," 22.

[40] Ibid.

[41] Ibid., 23.

[42] Lowrey, 60.

[43] "Task Force 58 Command Chronology, 24."

[44] Ibid., 24-25.

[45] Ibid., 25.

[46] Ibid.

[47] Ibid., 26.

[48] Ibid.

[49] Lowrey, 113.

[50] "Task Force 58 Command Chronology," 30.

[51] Ibid.

[52] Ibid., 2.

[53] Ibid., 37.

[54] "Task Force 58 Thoughts," 2.

[55] Ibid.

[56] Ibid.

[57] Mattis-Valenti interview.

[58] William Joseph Slim, *Defeat Into Victory* (London: Macmillan, 1986), 217.

[59] Lowrey, 96.

[60] Slim, *Defeat Into Victory,* 259.

[61] Ibid., 217-21, 258-270.

[62] Mattis-Valenti interview.

[63] B. P. Shillaber, "Grierson's Raid," *Journal of the United States Cavalry Association* 14, no. 52 (April 1904): 686.

[64] Gen Mattis's intent for Task Force 58 emailed to the author by Gen Mattis. Full intent can be found in Appendix A.

[65] Ibid.

[66] Richard W. Stewart, ed., *American Military History: The United States Army in a Global Era, 1917-2008*, 2nd ed. (Washington, DC: Center of Military History United States Army, 2010), 2:350.

[67] Lowrey, 96.

[68] Ibid.

[69] Mattis-Valenti interview.

[70] "Task Force 58 Thoughts," 3.

[71] Mattis-Valenti interview.

[72] Ibid.

CHAPTER 3

COMMANDING GENERAL 1ST MARINE DIVISION 2003

Overview

This chapter will analyze General Mattis's command of the 1st Marine Division in OIF I in 2003 and make comparisons to Task Force 58. Specifically staff structure, imaging the division through the first days of battle, logistics, and historical influences will show commonalities to Task Force 58. Task Force 58 was a formative base for his command of the 1st Marine Division.

Immediately after taking command of the 1st Marine Division, literally hours after the change of command ceremony, General Mattis began the process of transitioning the division from a peacetime force to one on a wartime footing. The general's purpose was clear: the division was getting ready to be part of the invasion of Iraq. General Mattis's commitment to this end was absolute as he stated, "Everything we do is to be focused on the destruction of the Iraqi Army. Everything. Anything that does not point us to that objective needs to be eliminated."[1] As an example, he eliminated extraneous reports, inspections, and conferences that wasted precious time and resources.

Staff Structure

The overall staff structure of the 1st Marine Division saw some similarities with that of the Task Force 58 staff in that every member was again expected to fill sandbags. General Mattis demanded "aggressive MAGTF officers" who were not merely "stove-piped experts" in their particular field or staff section.[2] This ensured that every member of the staff was multi-faceted and could aid in contributing much more to the division's overall mission. This aided when Mattis downsized the division command post (CP). Based on his previous experience with Task Force 58 he found a CP with a leaner staff and smaller footprint is more mobile and eliminates a bureaucratic atmosphere that is an impediment to faster execution and decision-making.

An important part of General Mattis's overall command climate was the relationship between the commanders and staff throughout the division. He stressed, "habitual relationships [between commanders and staff] were a conduit for speed."[3] Starting top down, Mattis created a "fraternity of shared risk and common vision."[4] His initial meetings with commanders and staff were likened to sweat lodge where "tribal chieftains [were] joining their tribes for battle."[5] He created an atmosphere where barriers between commanders and staff and officers and enlisted were broken down. Members of the division were "valued for the contribution of their talents rather than the rank on [their] collar."[6] Empowerment and trust was the bedrock of the command culture. Because the staff was small, Mattis was able to impart his intent and guidance on every member leaving flexibility for the Marines to make decisions and execute orders on their own authority. This created a culture where everyone's input was valued and sought after facilitating speed of information and execution which was critical in carrying out their mission.

Mattis employed a concept that he coined 'Eyes Officers' or 'Juliets' to help augment the communication flow on the battlefield. These Juliets reported only to him. They could quickly inform him of an exposed flank or a moral problem for example. This concept is much like the present concept of a directed telescope, where the commander appoints certain individuals to be his eyes and ears on the battlefield. Some of his Juliets

38

included the sergeant major and the chaplain. His purpose was not to undercut the chain of command, but rather build his situational awareness quickly in a developing situation. He stated that if a unit was in contact and taking casualties the commander was concerned with fighting his unit and communication to higher is lower on his priority list. He was aware of the possibility of undercutting the chain of command "with eyes officers running around. Commanders had to know that they were their friends. These were the guys that could get their ideas to me without going through the staff."[7] Thus, he opened up another avenue of communication and bypassed possible friction.

Concerning the formation of his staff, Mattis stated that he needed people that understood the way he thought.[8] The selection of Lieutenant Colonel Broadmeadow and Lieutenant Colonel Lethin as his G-4 and Deputy G-3 respectively, were evidence of this. Both of these Marines served on his Task Force 58 staff in those positions and their recent combat experience would serve his staff well. Furthermore, Mattis had a longstanding relationship with Lieutenant Colonel Lethin as he was his executive officer when Mattis commanded Marine Corps Recruiting Station Portland. General Mattis also convinced Captain Cook, his aide during Task Force 58, to stay on for another tour as his aide recalling that they had invaded two countries together.[9] These habitual relationships were key components of his staffing philosophy.

Some key members of his staff, in particular his G-4, were filled by personnel of lower rank than called for by the table of organization and equipment. The fact that there were lieutenant colonels filling colonel billets has given rise to the perception that General Mattis preferred lieutenant colonels on his staff vice colonels; this was not the case. During the time period the division prepared, there was a Marine Corps wide deficit of colonels. So Mattis did not prefer lieutenant colonels, it was more of a matter of "devolving to Lieutenant Colonels than preferring them."[10]

## Imaging

General Mattis believed that in order to generate speed, achieve depth in operations, and prepare for the uncertainty of battle, it was crucial that every member of the division understood explicitly the mission and the overarching commander's intent. He accomplished this through a process he called imaging. He wanted every Marine and Sailor in the division to be able to visualize everything from embarkation, planning, and deployment, to the first five days of combat. In order to accomplish this he personally briefed every member of the division on their mission and his commander's intent. This amounted to a ninety-minute briefing delivered to the units aimed at the lance corporal level. Over thirty briefings were given between October 10, 2002 and January 13, 2003. The results were positive with one lance corporal stating, "This was the only briefing the Marines ever sat through in an auditorium that they actually enjoyed."[11] The importance of commander's intent to the success of this operation cannot be overstated. The Marines knew they were going deep and it was quite possible that they would not be in constant contact with their commanders. "The commander's intent is the glue that holds [the division] together and ensures [the division] can achieve objectives beyond expectations."[12] A similar practice of personally delivering his intent to his subordinates was practiced in Task Force 58, but due to time constraints and the physical dispersion of his command, he was unable to meet with every subordinate.

While ensuring that nearly every member of the division understood the commander's intent, Mattis worked on the plan. In order to continue to image the intricate process coordinating the movement and logistics of 5,000 vehicles and 20,000 personnel, he wanted a hands on tactile experience.[13] After all, the push from Kuwait to the outskirts of Baghdad would be the longest Marine overland operation since 1805 when Lieutenant Presley O'Bannon led his Marines over 600 miles to attack the fortress at Derna, Tripoli.[14] General Mattis conceived of the Lego Drill to solve this problem.

Convoy and logistics planning is a difficult task under normal circumstances. The amount of vehicles and equipment necessary to keep the 1st Marine Division supplied during battle was vast and extremely complex. Equipment not only had to be prioritized but positioned within the order of march such that anticipated equipment would be readily available when needed. The potential for traffic jams and confusion due to the fog of war, friction, and enemy action was significant. To aid in the visualization of this complex operation and expand on the details of movement, General Mattis ordered the purchase of over 6,000 Lego blocks to represent each vehicle in the division. Each unit was assigned a color code and their appropriately colored Lego vehicles were mounted on a cardboard plate. The Legos were then placed on a scale terrain model located on the parade deck outside the division headquarters building on Camp Pendleton.

The first Lego drill took place on December 5, 2002, with each unit moving their Lego pieces as the division went through the scheme of maneuver. The Lego drill identified friction points that the staff were able to work through. Higher headquarters, the intelligence section, and General Mattis constantly refined the plan as the political and enemy situation were constantly changing. The division's forward CP was located in Kuwait and constantly sent refinements to their reach back cell at Camp Pendleton. A second Lego drill was conducted on January 10, 2003, at Camp Pendleton's Landing

41

Zone Horno. General Mattis flew back from his forward command post in Kuwait for each of these Lego drills with updates from the front.[15]

The Lego drill was a complex drill and it was difficult to establish a 'who's who' amongst the mass of Marines all clad in their identical desert camouflaged utilities. Keeping with the spirit of aggressive MAGTF officers, General Mattis's aide came up with the idea of outfitting the Marines with different colored numbered jerseys that corresponded to each unit's colors and unit identification. For example, 3rd Battalion, 5th Marines would wear a jersey with 5th Marines colors and the number thirty-five (see figure 6).

Figure 6.    Jersey Drill, LSA Matilda, Kuwait, February 27, 2003

*Source:* LtCol Michael S. Groen, *With the 1st Marine Division in Iraq, 2003: No Greater Friend, No Worse Enemy* (Quantico, VA: History Division Marine Corps University, 2006), 126.

Once jerseys were procured, they were flown forward along with the division's main CP. A team of Marines dug an eighty meter by eighty-meter terrain model. Each regimental commander laid out his task organization, mission, and scheme of maneuver while the respective battalion commanders walked through the terrain model effectively covering in detail the first ninety-six hours of combat operations. In attendance were MEF and division staff members. This first jersey drill conducted on February 7, 2003, contributed greatly to a shared situational awareness to all those that attended.[16]

A second jersey and Lego drill was conducted on February 27, 2003. This was the capstone event to the division's planning and preparation. The terrain model needed to be expanded. A team of engineers equipped with bulldozers dug out a 100 meter by 100 meter terrain model consisting of an angled sand table surface, multi-tiered amphitheater, and stadium type seating for key personnel (see figure 7). In attendance were the I MEF commander, Lieutenant General Conway and 3d Marine Air Wing commander Major General Amos, as well as various other ranking key individuals. At the conclusion of the rehearsal, Lieutenant General Conway addressed the group and notified them that the president had given the notification to attack into Iraq on order. This drill served as the last full-scale rehearsal prior to combat and marked the shift from preparation to anticipated combat operations.[17]

Figure 7.   The Mother of All Terrain Models

*Source:* LtCol Michael S. Groen, *With the 1st Marine Division in Iraq, 2003: No Greater Friend, No Worse Enemy* (Quantico, VA: History Division Marine Corps University, 2006), 127.

Achieving Speed through Logistics—'Logistics Light' Concept

Mattis stated that, "The division scheme of maneuver was based on the concept that speed equals success" and therefore a "rapid speed of advance became the metric that guided all of the division G-4s' preparations for combat."[18] In order to fully accomplish this end, the division logistics element had to transform itself similarly to the transformation that the division staff underwent. A cumbersome and expansive Logistics Operations Center (LOC) could impede the division's movement; the LOC had to become smaller, more agile, and better integrated into the division combat operations center.

At the start of the planning process, the LOC was composed of 120 Marines and Sailors, several tents, and multiple trucks to aid in its movement. Of critical importance, the LOC was separated from the division's combat operations center both functionally and physically.[19] If the bulk of the logistics section was moved to the division support area located in Camp Commando, Kuwait and used for reachback capabilities (i.e. requests for information could be sent back), a significant decrease in personnel and associated equipment would be realized. Utilizing this new concept the LOC shrank from 120 personnel to twenty-six. The new LOC construct was focused on current logistical operations; using the MAGTF officer/Marine concept personnel could speak to all manner of logistical needs. The smaller LOC was able to occupy a tent with direct access to the division COC and it put its G-4 watch officer in the COC directly behind the G-3 watch officer.[20] This effectively tied the logistics section to the hip of the operations section that would allow for increased situational awareness and a rapid logistical response capability.

However, the new structure of the LOC by itself was not enough to fully realize General Mattis's intent for responsive logistics. A concept of 'Logistics Light' evolved which incorporated numerous innovations that would make the division a leaner, faster organization. The first of these concepts was for members of the staff to think like a brigade sized element rather than a division.[21] The byproduct of incorporating this mental shift was speed. In order to think like a brigade staff however, the division had to physically become leaner. General Mattis set the living standard for the division to the 0311 (Marine rifleman military occupational specialty) lance corporal level. This meant that every Marine was expected to sleep on the deck, not in a cot. By the omission of cots alone, a savings of eight medium lift tactical vehicle equivalents were freed for other uses. General Mattis also expected that every member of the division would eat one hundred percent of issued meals; this meant that every single item in a Meal Ready to Eat was to be consumed, without exception.[22] This was important because food is fuel for the body and like fuel for vehicles, it could not be wasted.

The fuel consumption of the division's 5,000 vehicles was a significant logistical concern to General Mattis and his staff. Innovative efforts were taken to minimize fuel consumption at every opportunity. It was a courts martial offense to leave vehicles idling, wasting precious fuel. Vehicles were also fitted with gypsy racks that could carry an extra thirty gallons of fuel and additional food and water.[23] The division also carried fuel test kits in order to test and utilize captured enemy fuel stores if they became available. External fuel bladders were also added to M1A1 tanks and Assault Amphibian Vehicles that could further increase their range and lessen their dependence on logistical trains. In short, anything on the vehicles that was not needed for combat operations was taken off and left behind.[24]

The result of the logistical improvements greatly influenced the ability of the division to move quickly and achieve battlefield depth. This was due largely to the innovation and the attitude of the Marines involved. Lieutenant Colonel Broadmeadow recalled after the operation, "the [Marine Corps] supply support system was inadequate most times and a total failure at its worst."[25] For example, standards for requesting and conducting resupply were non-existent. Multiple non-compatible computer programs were utilized at different levels of supply. Connectivity was not always possible on the battlefield so requests for supplies, confirmation of receipt of supply requests, and in transit visibility of the supplies could not be tracked electronically. This led to little faith in the automated systems and caused the Marines to use workarounds such as 'yellow stickies' and handwritten notes. Lieutenant Colonel Broadmeadow concluded that it was only due to the "innovative tenacity" of the Marines that made logistics support for the division a success.[26]

## Historical Influence

In order to gain an appreciation of the terrain he would be fighting in, General Mattis turned to history. He mandated that every major and above in the division read Russel Braddon's *The Siege*. This book chronicled the exploits of the British Expeditionary Force during their campaign in Mesopotamia during World War I.[27] Mattis said that, "*The Siege* was one of the few books written about fighting in Iraq."[28] Historically, because of the inhospitable terrain, defenders had typically tied themselves to "key water and land approaches to Baghdad."[29] The Assistant Division Commander, Brigadier General John F. Kelly, summarized what Saddam Hussein may have thought the allied invasion would have looked like: "if the invasion continued it would follow the failed British 1915 example making its way along the Tigris River-Highway 6 corridor from Basra to Baghdad. [Saddam's] defensive dispositions certainly suggested this was his expectation."[30] In his operational design, General Mattis, along with I MEF, decided to bypass those units by attacking up Highways 1 and 7 vice Highway 6 (the eastern approach). It was necessary to threaten Baghdad quickly and prevent those units (the Iraqi IV Corps) from reinforcing Baghdad in order to enhance stabilization efforts (see figure 8).[31]

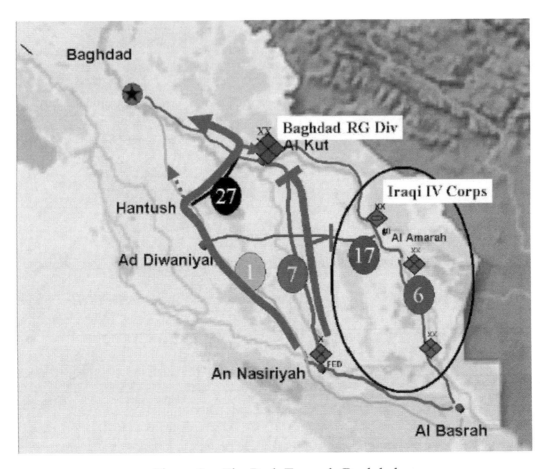

Figure 8.   The Push Towards Baghdad

*Source:* LtCol Michael S. Groen, *With the 1st Marine Division in Iraq, 2003: No Greater Friend, No Worse Enemy* (Quantico, VA: History Division Marine Corps University, 2006), 183.

General Mattis also studied *National Geographic* magazines to gain an appreciation for what would happen if the area between the Tigris and Euphrates Rivers flooded as it did in 1955.[32] If the Iraqis destroyed damns in the area then effects of the flood would be similar to that of the 1955 flood. He also studied Alexander the Great's movements throughout the area.[33]

A study of enemy commanders is an important part of General Mattis's operational art. He stated that, "if he could out fight their commanders then [he] wouldn't have to fight their troops."[34] He assigned a group of officers to study the Iraqi

commanders that he was likely to face. This may have been an influence from Slim.

During operations in Burma, Slim extensively studied the Japanese commanders he was

fighting against; even to go as far as hanging pictures of them above his desk.[35] Mattis

brought a retired Iraqi general to speak to his officers. This study did not have the effects

that he had hoped because there was little information about the Iraqi commanders he

would face. Nonetheless, the experience of study coupled with the information provided

by the Iraqi general confirmed some of their assumptions about the enemy.[36] In

maintaining the practice of studying enemy commanders, Mattis follows the teachings of

Sun Tzu, "When you are ignorant of the enemy but know yourself, your chances of

winning or losing are equal."[37]

## Conclusion

For General Mattis, a lean staff and small CP's generated speed on the battlefield

which translated into the division's ability to achieve physical depth in execution.

Because of refinements made to the physical size of the staff and the structure of the CP,

it was able to move throughout the battlefield quickly while constantly providing

command and control.

Imaging was a crucial part in the division's ability to generate speed and tempo on

the battlefield. Every Marine and Sailor in the division was familiar with General

Mattis's overall intent that allowed flexibility when battlefield friction set in. Friction

points were identified early on in the planning process and worked through with all

commanders present. The division's intense study of the scheme of maneuver allowed them to be more flexible when changes occurred because they were familiar with alternate courses of action.

The concept of Logistics Light enabled the division to travel great distances. In perhaps an earlier form of Logistics Light in Task Force 58, General Mattis decided not to take artillery to FOB Rhino because of the advances in combat aviation support. A single aircraft was now capable of attacking multiple targets during a single sortie. By not taking artillery into Rhino, it meant that he could bring more assault forces in the initial waves.[38] He used artillery in Iraq, but would have a bias for aviation fires because it meant less artillery rounds he would have to carry.[39]

As in Task Force 58, General Mattis's study of history influenced his operational art in Iraq. He was able to gain insights on the effects of terrain on his operations as well as likely enemy courses of action. General Mattis gained confidence in the distance he was able to achieve from his operations in Task Force 58 and stated, "he was unimpressed by the distance to Baghdad and beyond."[40]

General Mattis accepted risk by deciding not to secure all his lines of communication as he pressed forward in the attack. He expected every Marine to be a rifleman and expected that logistical resupply elements would sometimes have to "fight their way up to resupply the division's combat trains."[41] This would free up units otherwise dedicated to rear area security to provide maximum combat power in the attack, thus generating speed and tempo. He summed up his decision to accept risk by stating, "the more you strike deep against the enemy the more concern they have for their flanks and the less you have to have for yours."[42]

Speed was a necessary part of this operation because of the ground the division was fighting on and traveling through. When the Combined Forces Land Component Commander assigned the division its area of operations, the staff conducted a detailed terrain analysis. The analysis concluded that the majority the area of operations was "No Go" terrain because of a series of canals, drainage ditches, and untrafficable terrain.[43] This meant that the division's movement would be more or less restricted to roads. In order to keep pace with the other units on their flanks, the division had to ensure that it kept moving quickly. There was a threat that the Iraqis would attempt to flood the region by blowing damns. Speed of advance was necessary to deny the enemy that capability.[44] This speed of advance was made possible by the division's intense study of the scheme of maneuver through imaging. The speed of the staff process allowed any friction points to be quickly overcome.

[1] LtCol Michael S. Groen, *With the 1st Marine Division in Iraq, 2003: No Greater Friend, No Worse Enemy* (Quantico, VA: History Division Marine Corps University, 2006), 10.

[2] Ibid., 11.

[3] Ibid.

[4] Ibid., 12.

[5] Ibid.

[6] Ibid., 10.

[7] Mattis-Valenti interview.

[8] Ibid.

[9] Ibid.

[10] Mattis-Solis interview, 4.

[11] Groen, 38.

[12] LtCol Clarke R. Lethin, "1st Marine Division and Operation Iraqi Freedom," *Marine Corps Gazette* 88, no. 2 (February 2004): 22.

[13] Groen, 109.

[14] Michael R. Gordon and Bernard E. Trainor, *Cobra II: The Inside Story of the Invasion and Occupation of Iraq* (New York: Vintage Books, 2007), 209.

[15] Groen, 110-111.

[16] Ibid., 114-115.

[17] Ibid., 126.

[18] LtCol John J. Broadmeadow, "Logistics Support to 1st Marine Division During Operation Iraqi Freedom," *Marine Corps Gazette* 87, no. 8 (August 2003): 44.

[19] Ibid.

[20] Ibid.

[21] Groen, 11.

[22] Broadmeadow, 45.

[23] Mattis-Solis interview, 18.

[24] Groen, 3.

[25] Broadmeadow, 45.

[26] Ibid.

[27] Groen, 6.

[28] Mattis-Valenti interview.

[29] Groen, 180.

[30] BGen John F. Kelly, "Tikrit, South to Babylon," *Marine Corps Gazette* 88, no. 2 (February 2004): 16.

[31] Groen, 182-183.

[32] Mattis-Valenti interview.

[33] Ibid.

[34] Ibid.

[35] Slim, "Kermit Roosevelt Lecture."

[36] Mattis-Solis interview, 10.

[37] Sun Tzu, *The Art of War,* trans. Samuel B. Griffith (London: Oxford University Press, 1971), 84.

[38] Lowrey, 96.

[39] Groen, 4.

[40] Mattis-Solis interview, 22.

[41] Groen, 32.

[42] Mattis-Solis interview, 17.

[43] Groen, 6.

[44] Mattis-Valenti interview.

# CHAPTER 4

## COMMAND AND LEADERSHIP PHILOSOPHIES

### Overview

This chapter discusses General Mattis's command and leadership philosophies, in addition, a case study of leading in coalitions and team building will be analyzed that will see Mattis's philosophies put into action. The concepts of speed, harmony, commander's intent, and leadership form the bedrock of General Mattis's philosophy.

### Command and Leadership Philosophies

General Mattis's leadership encompasses many facets, the base of which has a strong spiritual undertone. In this case, the word spiritual does not refer to religion; instead, it refers to *esprit de corps*, a sense of cohesion and trust that creates a harmony on the battlefield. The "spirits of the Sailors and Marines are [the] first and last the real weapon that we have. With high spirits they can do anything . . . they will rapidly overcome any training deficiency . . . they'll find a way to get around the enemy . . . [they'll] create a sense of harmony that nothing can stop."[1]

Harmony is another key aspect of his leadership base. Harmony starts with the familiarity and cohesiveness of a unit. A unit gains familiarity, harmony, and cohesion by training together, experiencing hardships, and trusting each other. Measures must be taken to preserve the harmony and cohesiveness of a unit. He cites the greatest threat to the Marine Corps is not the enemy, but "a leader who is not admired . . . [Leaders] that earn the trust and respect of their subordinates, peers, and superiors, but also the affection of their subordinates."[2] Admired leaders create harmony in their units.

For example, just before 1st Marine Division was about to deploy for OIF, one of the company commanders received orders to Marine Security Guard Duty. General Mattis denied his orders and transfer under the pretense of harmony stating that, "I really wanted him with us because I really value cohesion and trust; habitual relationships and friendships when we go into a fight."[3] The Marine later executed his orders to Marine Security Guard Duty when the situation allowed it.

Preserving the integrity of a unit is paramount for cohesion. General Mattis uses a football analogy to highlight this. A football team would never be sent to play in the Super Bowl with an adhoc assortment of players that have not practiced and played together. The results would be disastrous. He believes that a similar situation on the battlefield (a non-cohesive adhoc assortment of strangers attempting to fight together) would lead to casualties, as arguably may have been the case in certain instances in Vietnam.[4] "It's all built on a basis; on a grounding of the spirits of the Marines and their willingness to go against the enemy with the people that are working alongside them."[5]

Mattis embraced General John A. Lejeune's philosophy that the "relation between officers and enlisted men should in no sense be that of superior and inferior nor that of master and servant, but rather that of teacher and scholar. In fact, it should partake of the nature of the relation between father and son, to the extent that officers, especially commanding officers, are responsible for the physical, mental, and moral welfare, as well as the discipline and military training of the young men under their command."[6] In his relationships, General Mattis preferred the term coaching rather than commanding.[7] He commented that only about fifteen minutes a day was needed to command and the rest of the time he was coaching and setting conditions where his units could succeed.[8]

Mattis believes in delegating responsibility to the lowest capable level. He stated, "Most Marine units and most Marines can do more than they are asked to do. It's how you unleash that, delegate the decision making to the lowest capable level so that units can maneuver swiftly and aggressively based on exercising initiative. A sense of co-equal ownership of the mission between Generals and 18 year olds."[9] He goes on to explain that commanders that know history and have trust in their subordinates are the key to unleashing initiative.

It is imperative that communication is fostered in a command environment. General Mattis used Hegel's Dialectic as a method to communicate with his staff. Hegel's Dialectic operates by proposing a thesis, then stating the antithesis and from the two a synthesis is reached. Clausewitz's *On War* is an example of a book that is written in Hegel's Dialectic. Mattis spent most of his time in combat with lead units. When he came back from the front, he briefed his staff on the events as he saw them. His staff would then brief the events from their point of view. From this interchange of thesis and antithesis, a synthesis was obtained. This led to more accurate and faster decision making which was brought to bear against the enemy.[10] This plays into Mattis's generalization that there are two kinds of general officers: ones that are briefed by their staff and ones that brief their staffs on events.[11]

In the 1st Marine Division during Mattis's command, speed was a culture. Speed "was a way of thinking—the mental gymnastics we have to do to solve a problem quickly and efficiently."[12] In order to be able to operate in an operational design centered on cutting the enemy off from his logistics and command and control, required the division's units to move their personnel and equipment simultaneously.[13] This was realized when,

56

in response to a change in the enemy situation, "Regimental Combat Team (RCT) 5 was able to attack from a standing start within 5 hours of notification—a dawn attack modified into a night attack."[14]

Marine Corps Doctrinal Publication 1, *Warfighting,* defines speed as a "rapidity of action. It applies to both time and space. Speed over time is tempo—the consistent ability to operate quickly."[15] The steps of the Boyd Cycle or OODA Loop are: Observe, Orient, Decide, and Act. An orientation (think of it as an estimate of the situation) to an observation is made; a decision is contemplated and then put into action.[16] Every iteration of this cycle keeps the enemy one step behind, observing and orienting on past actions while new decisions and actions are being implemented. This will ultimately lead to the enemy becoming "less effective until, finally, he is overcome by events."[17]

Mattis describes the importance of speed and alludes to the Boyd Cycle when he comments that speed encompasses:

> information passing, speed of logistics resupply, speed of assembly area operations, speed of getting orders out to people. But speed in itself creates a dilemma for the enemy because even if they're reacting to what you're doing, if you're already doing something else, he's got another problem. And you keep doing this faster and faster so long as you don't lose your own basic harmony. [It's] based on implicit communications. It's based on trust, knowledge of each other, cohesion.[18]

Mattis uses commander's intent to increase speed on the battlefield by personally articulating it to his subordinates.

### The Importance of Commander's Intent

Marine Corps Doctrinal Publication 1 defines commander's intent as "a device designed to help subordinates understand the larger context of their actions."[19] It goes on to further explain the purpose of commander's intent as allowing "subordinates to exercise judgment and initiative—to depart from the original plan when the unforeseen occurs—in a way that is consistent with higher commanders' aims."[20] Commander's intent is the cornerstone for General Mattis's style of warfare. It "focuses decisive action at the right time and place; not the centralized, command by plan/command by direction, systems-focused processes that require subordinates to request permission before taking action."[21]

Intent is a method in which aggressiveness can be unleashed.[22] It is generally the only part of plan that survives first contact; therefore, it is imperative that the "inventiveness, creativity and adaptability of subordinate leaders"[23] are not stifled by blind adherence to a plan that has met the enemy's opposing will.

Battalion command is most likely the last time that all of the men under one's command are recognized. As rank and responsibility is increased, a more articulate commander's intent is needed.[24] Commander's intent should be written so that it is timeless and enduring. In order to do this, a deep understanding of the situation is necessary. This can be linked back to speed, for if units are able to act rapidly within the commander's intent, the operation would be over faster thereby reducing casualties.[25] Shared situational understanding, commander's intent, and decentralized implementation "enable us to place an adversary on the horns of a dilemma that overwhelms him through cascading tactical events that collapse his will to fight."[26]

So critical was the commander's intent to the success of operations that before the 1st Marine Division crossed the line of departure in their march to Baghdad in 2003, General Mattis delivered his commander's intent personally to every Marine and Sailor in the division. Every word and sentence in the intent was intentionally crafted to carry weight and meaning. "Equally important to the commander giving the intent was the division staff fully understanding the intent."[27] Speed and efficiency were capitalized on because of the effort and care that was taken to make sure the intent was understood by all. Over thirty fragmentary orders were issued during the push to Baghdad with all. As a testament to the understanding of the intent and the staff processes that were in place, transitions between planners and operators were as seamless "as you could find on that chaotic battlefield."[28]

## Command and Control

General Mattis has said that he does not use command and control, he uses command and feedback.[29] He was not interested in controlling units because opportunities on the battlefield presented by the enemy are fleeting. The only way to capitalize on these opportunities is to understand and work within the constraints of the commander's intent using speed and decisive action.[30] His understanding of command and control is "command [is] the exercise of authority, and control [is] the feedback generated by decision implementation."[31]

To General Mattis, command and control is all about communication and coordination up and down the chain of command and laterally between units. To emphasize this point, General Mattis discusses situations where fire support coordination measures can favor the enemy and decrease speed and tempo in operations. The enemy will not always agree with the placement of fire support coordination measures on a map and generally will try to exploit them. If few fire support coordination measures or boundaries are placed on the map, it necessitates communication and coordination between commanders. One could argue that this coordination would have happened anyway because of the fire support coordination measures, but now commanders are coordinating on boundaries that make sense to them on the ground they are on. He views that this can increase speed and flexibility because all courses of action are open and not hampered by the pretext that "I can't go that way, because I don't own the ground."[32] Coordinating over a line on the ground that was put there before the enemy got a vote could adversely affect speed.[33] It is recognized that this practice is controversial and might even introduce more friction or even fratricide, but it was a lesson learned when Mattis was in command of 7th Marines. The takeaway is that coordination should take place constantly and that a line on the ground should not impede initiative.

Mattis's command and control philosophy is best summarized by the way he used it in Task Force 58. He issued broad intent and made sure his staff set the conditions for which the two MEUs could succeed. He empowered his subordinate commanders to enable them what they knew how to do best: command their units. In OIF, his philosophy was similar. He placed himself at the point of friction and observed if his intent was being carried out. He was in a position where he could adjust intent if the situation dictated it. He could also ensure that his intent was being met, and if not, take appropriate measures to rectify the situation.

<u>Professional Military Education</u>

Perhaps one of the greatest influences on General Mattis's operational art and leadership is the value he places on the importance of independent study and learning. He urges warriors to have a "professional curiosity that will carry them beyond institutional learning."[34] This statement is profound and bolsters the notion of the military being a profession.[35] A commitment to lifelong learning is essential as a member of the military grows intellectually and professionally.

Mattis asserts that "by reading, you learn through others' experiences—generally a better way to do business—especially in our line of work where the consequences of incompetence are so final for young men."[36] This alludes to a responsibility that is inherent to commanders and leaders: honest and detailed preparation for the task. It goes far beyond just concentrating study on tactics, techniques, and procedures, for that will never be enough for "those who must adapt to overcoming an independent enemy's will are not allowed the luxury of ignorance of their profession."[37]

War is a human endeavor[38] and as such, warriors must be comfortable operating on and within the scopes of human terrain. An object in war is to impose our will upon the enemy.[39] It is critical in professional study to include the study of the human dimension that is the study of decision-making, group interaction, leadership, etc. When the enemy votes a study of these topics will enable the warrior to beat him to the polls.

As alluded to in previous chapters, General Mattis has used history as an intellectual stepping stone for his operational design and art or as he dubs it the "practice of informed boldness."[40] As proof to his theory that understanding history "means that we face nothing new under the sun,"[41] Mattis explains "Alexander the Great would not be in the least bit perplexed by the enemy that we face right now in Iraq."[42] The consequences are dire if commanders and leaders shirk this responsibility. As General Mattis testifies, he believes that "many of [his] young guys lived because [he] didn't waste their lives because [he] didn't have the vision in [his] mind of how to destroy the enemy at the least cost to our guys and to innocents on the battlefield."[43]

The study of history, in particular in this case, the study of military history can be viewed as a starting point for professional military education. While it will not always give all the answers, it will "[light] what is often a dark path ahead."[44] Taken in context with the realization that history will not and does not repeat itself, past situations can serve as a cognitive framework for the innovative solutions to modern problem sets. Using this technique, Mattis recalls that he has "never been caught flatfooted by any situation, and [he's] never been at a loss for how any problem has been addressed (successfully or unsuccessfully) before."[45]

It is important to note that failure when utilizing this method will sometimes occur and that failure should not be frowned upon but should be encouraged. To have a repository of solutions to problems in the mind and have the fear of failure stifle initiative is just as detrimental. Commanders and leaders must cultivate a culture where failure is encouraged so that mistakes can be learned from. To put it into context of expeditionary operations in support of combatant commander problem sets, Mattis states that, "we need to push the envelope in our exercises and be unconcerned with failure as we create operational answers to COCOM problems by imaginative employment of Navy-Marine expeditionary forces."[46]

### Building a Coalition Case Study—Philosophies Put into Action

During the planning for and the execution of Task Force 58's mission, General Mattis quite often found himself lacking in resources, capabilities, and relative authority. Compensating for these lacks was accomplished by building coalitions through personal relationships. As a matter of context, coalition in this case includes joint and interagency partners.

When General Mattis and his staff found themselves quickly outgrowing their spaces in Bahrain, he decided to move to a vacant lot. He contacted SEABEES from Naval Mobile Construction Battalion 133 who, in the course of just five days, erected three concrete pads, three tents, and surrounded the new area with concertina wire.[47] Mattis was impressed with the spirit and accomplishment of the SEABEES that led him to request SEABEE support for Task Force 58 in Afghanistan. The SEABEES in Afghanistan were the only reason Rhino was a success. Under extremely austere conditions and with little resources, they were able to keep the runway usable for fixed wing aircraft like the venerable Marine KC-130 and Air Force C-17. The SEABEES also improved sanitary conditions on the FOB. They proved to be true combat multipliers.[48]

Mattis also formed a close relationship with Task Force 57, a US Navy P-3 aircraft squadron specializing in reconnaissance. He and some of his staff would fly on the P-3s over objectives in Afghanistan to get a bird's eye view of the situation. It was during one of his first flights that he realized he could "accelerate the enemy's downfall by seizing a stronghold to their rear and [force] a turning movement."[49] This was the genesis for the seizure of Rhino. Mattis was so impressed with their capabilities that he would use them extensively in Afghanistan and again in Iraq for airborne reconnaissance and command and control.

Another instance of "HANDCON" (informal command relationships agreed on by the commanders involved) was the relationship formed with Naval Special Warfare Group 1. Their commander, Captain Robert S. Harward, was a student at the Naval Academy Preparatory School when General Mattis was a battalion officer. General Mattis met with Captain Harward briefly at Naval Amphibious Base Coronado. After a meeting with Admiral Moore on October 31, 2001, General Mattis was walking to his

quarters in Bahrain when he noticed Captain Harward standing under a street light.

Harward was forming what would become Task Force K-Bar and when Mattis asked

what he was doing, Harward replied, "I'm trying to get into the fight, but I don't have any

helicopters."[50] Mattis jumped at the opportunity and over a handshake, he agreed to

provide the SEALS with lift capable in return for strategic reconnaissance of Task Force

Objectives. The SEALS from Task Force K-Bar were in place at Rhino four days before

the assault and provided the Task Force 58 staff with intelligence and aided in the landing

of the first assault waves. Mattis also traded liaison officers with the SEALS.

It was apparent to Mattis that today's operations move at the speed of trust.[51]

Mattis believed that there was a job for everyone when it came to operations involving

joint and coalition forces and had two perquisites for them: they must be interoperable

and they must possess tactical mobility.[52] In order to solve issues of interoperability,

Mattis turned to the heavy use of liaison officers. Speaking on the type of commander of

various units, Mattis details that anything is possible with the right attitude. "If they're

the kind you want to make happen there's no reason to be concerned about whether or not

you have the right radios or anything else. If you want to make it happen just put a liaison

officer in each other's CPs with their own radios so you can talk back and forth and get

on with killing people."[53] It is about commander's relationships, not command

relationships states Mattis referring to Bruce Catton's book, *Grant Takes Command*.[54]

Mattis asserts that a commander must "be ready to embrace allied elements

without necessarily having TACON/OPCON over them—use HANDCON."[55] Bringing

allied elements into the planning process early with an emphasis on information sharing a commander can gain battlefield harmony through trust building.[56] His bottom line is that "you will have little formal authority yet expectations for tactical achievements will not be diminished just because you lack formal command authority."[57]

The greatest attribute a field grade officer can have according to Mattis is anticipation.[58] General Mattis anticipated his lack of resources, capabilities, and authorities and actively sought measures to correct them by forming relationships and exchanging liaison officers.

## Conclusion

According to Mattis, "command is all about leadership and self-confidence."[59] Commanders should only use force of personality against the enemy and need to have compassion for the Marines they lead.[60] A sense of humor is included in compassion. He comments, "a sense of humor is like body armor around your body. It's armor around your spirit and it keeps your spirit from going grim."[61] Grim refers to the sometimes-unthinkable tasks one has to accomplish in combat.

The concepts of speed and harmony when used in concert with a strong commander's intent will carry the day. It is the commander's responsibility to set conditions where speed and initiative can be brought to bear against the enemy. Speed not only linked to movement, but flow of information and decision-making. Using these principles in conjunction with applied leadership and an atmosphere of trust he proved that there is nothing his Marines could not accomplish.

---

[1] Mattis-Solis interview, 53.

[2] Mattis-Valenti interview.

[3] Mattis-Solis inerview, 8.

[4] Ibid., 9.

[5] Ibid.

[6] Headquarters United States Marine Corps, *Marine Corps Manual w/ CH 1-3,* (Washington, DC: United States Marine Corps, 1980), 1-22.

[7] Mattis-Kreisler interview.

[8] Ibid.

[9] Mattis-Valenti interview.

[10] Mattis-Kreisler interview.

[11] Ibid.

[12] Lethin, 21.

[13] Ibid.

[14] Ibid.

[15] United States Marine Corps, Marine Corps Doctrinal Publication (MCDP) 1, *Warfighting* (Washington, DC: Headquarters United States Marine Corps, 1997), 40.

[16] Ibid., 102-103.

[17] Ibid. 103

[18] Mattis-Solis interview, 28.

[19] United States Marine Corps, MCDP 1, 89.

[20] Ibid.

[21] LtGen James N. Mattis, "Commanding General's Command and Control (C2) Intent," *Marine Corps Gazette* 90, no. 8 (August 2006): 16.

[22] Mattis-Kreisler interview.

[23] Mattis, "Commanding General's Command and Control (C2) Intent," 16.

[24] Mattis-Kreisler interview.

[25] Mattis-Solis interview, 29.

[26] Mattis, "Commanding General's Command and Control (C2) Intent," 16.

[27] Lethin, 22.

[28] Ibid., 21.

[29] Mattis-Kreisler interview.

[30] Ibid.

[31] Mattis, "Commanding General's Command and Control (C2) Intent," 16.

[32] Mattis-Solis interview, 24-25.

[33] Ibid.

[34] Mattis-Kreisler interview.

[35] SgtMaj James D. Willeford, "What Is a Military Professional?: Do we have a professional enlisted corps?," *Marine Corps Gazette* 98, no. 9 (September 2014): 95-96.

[36] MajGen James N. Mattis, "The Professional Edge," *Marine Corps Gazette* 88, no. 2 (February 2004): 19.

[37] Ibid., 20.

[38] Carl von Clausewitz, *On War,* trans. Michael Howard, Peter Paret, and Bernard Brodie (Princeton, NJ: Princeton University Press, 1984), 86.

[39] Ibid., 75.

[40] "Task Force 58 Thoughts," 2.

[41] Mattis, "The Professional Edge," 19.

[42] Ibid. Also note that the time period referenced was circa 2003-2004 in Iraq.

[43] Ibid., 20.

[44] Ibid., 19.

[45] Ibid.

[46] "Task Force 58 Thoughts," 3.

[47] Lowrey, 82.

[48] Ibid., 125-126.

[49] Ibid., 97.

[50] Mattis-Solis interview, 47-48.

[51] Mattis-Kreisler interview.

[52] Lowrey, 91.

[53] Mattis-Solis interview, 50.

[54] Mattis, "The Professional Edge," 20.

[55] "Task Force 58 Thoughts," 5.

[56] Ibid., 6.

[57] Ibid.

[58] Mattis-Solis interview, 11.

[59] Ibid.

[60] Ibid.

[61] Mattis-Kreisler interview.

# CHAPTER 5

## CONCLUSIONS AND RECOMMENDATIONS

### Conclusions

General Mattis remains one of the most iconic Marines of recent decades as a result of his accomplishments as the commander of Task Force 58 and later the 1st Marine Division in OIF I. He proved a flexible general officer capable of operating in any clime and place. As demonstrated in Afghanistan as the commander of Task Force 58 he was able to quickly and effectively integrate two disparate units into a single capable combat force. He ably employed that force deep in enemy territory, with minimal planning time and resources, and to devastating effects.

Less than one year after his command of Task Force 58, General Mattis was in command of the 1st Marine Division. Immediately upon taking command, he began preparation for combat operations in Iraq that later concluded in the "longest sequence of coordinated overland attacks in the history of the Corps."[1] The lessons and experiences from Task Force 58, in particular the distance and depth achieved, left him "unimpressed by the distance to Baghdad and beyond."[2]

### Historical Influences on Decision Making

Mattis informs his decision-making by using historical examples as a framework for informed options. His vast knowledge of history coupled with personal experiences generates a tempo and speed in his own decision-making. Some decisions can be made on informed instinct rather than a quantitative decision making process.[3] Using history as a background, he is able to size up the situation and then evaluate courses of action. This lends to Dr. Gary Klein's Recognition-Primed Decision Model.[4] For Mattis, history serves as the mental stimulation that increases his situational awareness and influences his decision-making.[5] This concept is in line with Clausewitz's definition of *coup d'oeil*: "the quick recognition of a truth that the mind would ordinarily miss or would perceive only after long study and reflection."[6]

Mattis places a high priority on reading and reflection of the profession of arms. He states, "The Marine Corps could explain to you how to fight, but they can't comprehend it for you, you've got to be the one who takes a responsibility for it."[7] Mattis saw his responsibility started with reading the Commandant's reading list. He humbly states that he "was a pretty average Marine, any Marine General could have done [what he did] as long as they did their homework and didn't contract out their thinking."[8]

<u>Leadership and Command Philosophies</u>

General Mattis's leadership and command philosophies seemed to be constant throughout these two periods of combat. Both his leadership and command philosophies aimed at creating an environment of chaos in which the enemy could not thrive, but his Marines could. He accomplished this through both mental and physical means. Mentally he prepared his Marines for the rigors of combat by emphasizing battlefield harmony and promoting professional military education through a rigorous study of history and leadership. Physically he constrained the size of his staffs, developed a logistics concept that would allow him to achieve unprecedented depth on the battlefield, solicited aggressive MAGTF officers, developed command and control systems that could support rapidly changing situations, and issued durable commander's intent aimed at providing subordinate commanders maximum flexibility in the accomplishment of their assigned missions.

## The Mattis Way of War

A common theme emerged amongst his commands of Task Force 58 and 1st Marine Division in OIF I that was evident in his leadership and command philosophies: speed. Not speed as defined by distance over time, but speed of information flow, decision making, violence of action, and orders production and execution. He used speed to out cycle in the OODA loop sense (OODA as in Observe, Orient, Decide, and Act). Using speed as a common metric, the Mattis Way of War can be explained.

General Mattis creates a potential energy bolstered on pillars of command and control, commander's intent, logistics light concept,[9] Professional military education, historical influences, liaison officers, small staffs, battlefield harmony, and leadership. This potential energy can be quickly transferred to kinetic energy (read from capability to action) which translates to speed. When the action is met by enemy reaction, it has enough force to impart his will on the enemy by creating a chaotic environment with which the enemy cannot cope. The speed and violence of action has a component of width associated with it that allows for flexibility because of the enemy's will. This 'width' is bounded by commander's intent and allows subordinate commanders freedom of action in the accomplishment of their mission in the face of an opposing will (see figure 9).

Another way to grasp figure 9 is to think of a marble (representing the unit) perched on top of the pillars of commander's intent, command and control, history, liaison officers, and small staff. These pillars are bound by speed, leadership, harmony, and feedback. The marble now possesses potential energy and has built up capacity. When the marble is released, it rolls down the ramp that is bounded by the commander's intent (signifying that there is flexibility in the path). Its capacity is transferred from potential to kinetic energy where it interacts with the enemy's will. The marble then rebounds because of its momentum and increases its potential. It then can be unleashed (transfer of potential to kinetic) again. This process is repeated until culmination and then recharged.

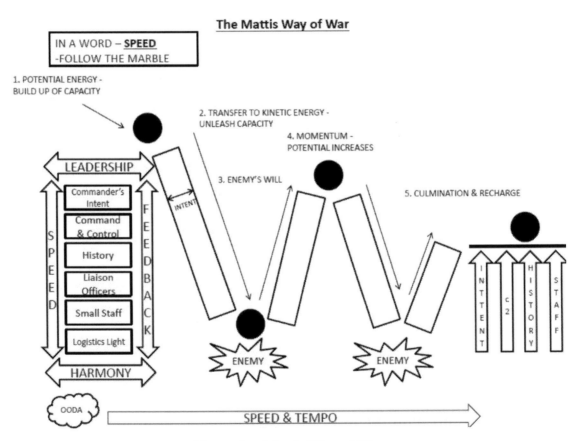

Figure 9.   Mattis Way of War

*Source:* Created by author.

## Innovations as Paradigm Shifts

Mattis's unique innovations in Task Force 58 and the 1st Marine Division such as Skip Echelon, applying historical influences to operational design, the Jersey and Lego drills, and Logistics Light concepts constitute paradigm shifts. He was able to think and innovate beyond current constructs and apply new methods that did not fit in current methodologies. By doing this, he has created new paradigms that will inspire further changes to a commander's operational art and design.[10]

Every action and preparation taken by Mattis generates speed and tempo. Whether it was the command and control construct he established between the 15th and 26th MEU in Task Force 58 or the Jersey Drills conducted in preparation to image combat operations in OIF I. They all enabled the unit to operate faster than the enemy could cope with. The generation of speed is the bedrock for the Mattis Way of War that allowed him to achieve unprecedented depth on the field of battle.

## Recommendations for Further Study

The research conducted for this thesis has shed light on further areas of study that would benefit the military scholar. The following list of questions and topics serve as possible research questions that could be addressed in future works and studies.

A study of General Mattis's contribution to counterinsurgency doctrine. Starting with an examination of his operational art in OIF II to build a base and referencing current and contemporary counterinsurgency doctrine. Did he build off the US Marine Corps *Small Wars Manual* or did he implement a new approach? Was his approach successful in OIF II and would that approach have been successful in future iterations of Operation Enduring Freedom? When General Mattis was the Commanding General of

Marine Corps Combat Development Command, did he transplant his counterinsurgency experience into Marine Corps doctrine?

A study of what can be called the interwar periods of Mattis. What positions did he hold and what experiences were gained in between his combat operations during the Gulf War, Task Force 58, and OIF I? How did these experiences affect his judgment and leadership in the following conflicts and operations?

A comparison between the operational art of the 1st Marine Division in OIF I and that of the British Expeditionary Force in their exploits in Mesopotamia in 1914. What are the similarities and differences? Did we learn from past experiences? Did the Iraqis learn from their past?

Was the Mattis Way of War adapted by other Marine Corps units or other services? Will this way of war work in current conflicts and or larger scale more conventional future wars? What has to be adapted to effectively fight future wars? Can this way of war be applied to other domains such as cyber?

The generalship of Mattis while serving as Commanding General of Marine Corps Combat Development Command and CENTCOM. Did he grow as a general officer? Were his experiences as the Commanding General of Task Force 58 and Commanding General of the 1st Marine Division evident in his leadership in these positions? Did his practices influence or change doctrine? Do we as a Marine Corps fight differently because of him?

---

[1] Groen, iii.

[2] Mattis-Solis interview, 22.

[3] Maj Christopher J. Kirk, "The Demise of Decision Making: How Information Superiority Degrades Our Ability to Make Decisions," */luce.nt/ A Journal of National Security Studies* (Fall 2014): 84-93, accessed October 30, 2014, https://www.usnwc.edu/Publications/-Luce-nt-/Current/Pdfs/Kirk_The-Demise-of-Decision-Making-Colbert_Kirk-C-.aspx. Ideas from this article were taken to relate General Mattis's use of historical influences to informed options. The article further goes on to relate the use of Dr. Gary Klein's Recognition Primed Decision Model.

[4] Gary A. Klein, *Sources of Power: How People Make Decisions* (Cambridge, MA: MIT Press, 1998), 10.

[5] Ibid., 89-109. I am taking the ideas from Klein that make up his Recognition Prime-Primed Decision Making Model and using the information found in this chapter to draw out the correlation that history fills in for experience in Mattis's operational art.

[6] Clausewitz, 102.

[7] Mattis-Valenti interview.

[8] Ibid.

[9] The logistics light concept was brought to the attention of the author for inclusion in the pillars from an email conversation with Gen Mattis.

[10] Thomas S. Kuhn, *The Structure of Scientific Revolutions,* 4th ed. (Chicago: The University of Chicago Press, 2012), 10-18, 43-51. This book is used to create a reference for paradigm shifts that can be used to categorize Gen Mattis's innovations.

# GLOSSARY

Action Phase. In amphibious operations, the period of time between the arrival of the landing forces of the amphibious force in the operational area and the accomplishment of their mission.[1]

Aerial Refueling. The use of aerial tanker-configured aircraft to provide refueling service to helicopters, fixed-wing, and tilt-rotor aircraft in flight. Aerial refueling extends the range, time on station, mobility, and flexibility of Marine air-ground task force aircraft.[2]

Air Delivery. Air delivery is the transportation of equipment and supplies to Forward Operating Bases (FOBs) or remote areas. Delivery can be accomplished with helicopters or loads can be air dropped from fixed wing aircraft such as the KC-130. Air drops are normally used when surface or helicopter transports cannot be used because of range, closed lines of communications, a lack of adequate airfields, a prohibitive ground tactical situation, high tonnage, or reduced response time.[3]

Air Evacuation. Air evacuation is the transportation of personnel and equipment from Forward Operating Bases (FOBs) or remote areas. This includes flights from areas of operations to secure rear areas, medical evacuations, and extraction of forces. Transport helicopters and fixed-wing transport aircraft perform air evacuations.[4]

Air Logistical Support. Air logistical support operations are conducted by fixed-wing aircraft and provide assault support of MAGTF forces on the ground. Air logistical support delivers troops, equipment, and supplies to areas beyond helicopter range and lift capability or when surface transportation is slow or unavailable.[5]

Air Reconnaissance. The acquisition of information by employing visual observation and/or sensors in air vehicles. Air reconnaissance is one of the six Marine aviation functions.[6]

Amphibious Operation. A military operation launched from the sea by an amphibious force, embarked in ships or craft with the primary purpose of introducing a landing force ashore to accomplish the assigned mission.[7]

Antiair Warfare. That action required to destroy or reduce to an acceptable level the enemy air and missile threat. Antiair warfare integrates all offensive and defensive actions against enemy aircraft, surface-to-air weapons, and theater missiles into a singular, indivisible set of operations. Antiair warfare is one of the six functions of Marine aviation. Also called AAW.[8]

Assault Support. The use of aircraft to provide tactical mobility and logistic support for the Marine air-ground task force, the movement of high priority cargo and personnel within the immediate area of operations, in-flight refueling, and the evacuation of personnel and cargo. Assault support is one of the six functions of Marine aviation.[9]

Aviation Combat Element (ACE). The core element of a Marine air-ground task force (MAGTF) that is task-organized to conduct aviation operations. The aviation combat element (ACE) provides all or a portion of the six functions of Marine aviation necessary to accomplish the MAGTF's mission. These functions are antiair warfare, offensive air support, assault support, electronic warfare, air reconnaissance, and control of aircraft and missiles. The ACE is usually composed of an aviation unit headquarters and various other aviation units or their detachments. It can vary in size from a small aviation detachment of specifically required aircraft to one or more Marine aircraft wings. In a joint or multinational environment, the ACE may contain other Service or multinational forces assigned or attached to the MAGTF. The ACE itself is not a formal command. Also called ACE.[10]

Battlefield Illumination (BI). Battlefield illumination can be provided by both fixed-wing and rotary-wing aircraft. Illumination may be visible to the naked eye or invisible (i.e., visible only with night vision equipment). Battlefield illumination can last for a few minutes or several hours.[11]

Combat Assault Support. Provides mobility and logistic support to the MAGTF. It is used to deploy forces efficiently in offensive maneuver warfare, bypass obstacles, or quickly redeploy forces. Combat assault support allows the MAGTF commander to build up his forces rapidly at a specific time and location.[12]

Control of Aircraft and Missiles. The coordinated employment of facilities, equipment, communications, procedures, and personnel that allows the aviation combat element commander to plan, direct, and control the efforts of the aviation combat element to support the accomplishment of the Marine air-ground task force mission. Control of aircraft and missiles is one of the six functions of Marine aviation.[13]

Electronic Warfare. EW is any military action involving the use of electromagnetic and directed energy to control the electromagnetic spectrum or to attack the enemy. EW supports the warfighting functions of fires, command and control, and intelligence through the three major subdivisions:, electronic attack, electronic protection, and electronic warfare support.[14]

Embarkation Phase. In amphibious operations, the phase that encompasses the orderly assembly of personnel and materiel and their subsequent loading aboard ships and/or aircraft in a sequence designed to meet the requirements of the landing force concept of operations ashore.[15]

Marine Air Ground Task Force (MAGTF). The Marine Corps' principal organization for all missions across a range of military operations, composed of forces task-organized under a single commander capable of responding rapidly to a contingency anywhere in the world. The types of forces in the Marine air-ground task force (MAGTF) are functionally grouped into four core elements: a command element, an aviation combat element, a ground combat element, and a logistics combat element. The four core elements are categories of forces, not formal commands. The basic structure of the MAGTF never varies, though the number, size, and type of Marine Corps units comprising each of its four elements will always be mission dependent. The flexibility of the organizational structure allows for one or more subordinate MAGTFs to be assigned. In a joint or multinational environment, other Service or multinational forces may be assigned or attached. Also called MAGTF.[16]

Marine Aviation Functions. The six functions (antiair warfare, offensive air support, assault support, electronic warfare, air reconnaissance, and control of aircraft and missiles) performed by Marine aviation in support of the Marine air-ground task force.[17]

Marine Expeditionary Unit (MEU). A Marine air-ground task force (MAGTF) that is constructed around an infantry battalion reinforced, a composite squadron reinforced, and a task-organized logistics combat element. It normally fulfills Marine Corps' forward sea-based deployment requirements. The Marine expeditionary unit provides an immediate reaction capability for crisis response and is capable of limited combat operations. In a joint or multinational environment, it may contain other Service or multinational forces assigned or attached to the MAGTF. Also called MEU.[18]

Movement Phase. In amphibious operations, the period during which various elements of the amphibious force move from points of embarkation to the operational area. This move may be via rehearsal, staging, or rendezvous areas. The movement phase is completed when the various elements of the amphibious force arrive at their assigned positions in the operational area.[19]

Offensive Air Support. Those air operations conducted against enemy installations, facilities, and personnel to directly assist the attainment of MAGTF objectives by the destruction of enemy resources or the isolation of the enemy's military forces. Offensive air support is one of the six functions of Marine aviation. Also called OAS.[20]

Planning Phase. In amphibious operations, the phase normally denoted by the period extending from the issuance of the initiating directive up to the embarkation phase. The planning phase may occur during movement or at any other time upon receipt of a new mission or change in the operational situation.[21]

Rehearsal Phase. In amphibious operations, the period during which the prospective operation is practiced for the purpose of: (1) testing adequacy of plans, the timing of detailed operations, and the combat readiness of participating forces; (2) ensuring that all echelons are familiar with plans; and (3) testing communications-information systems.[22]

Tactical Recovery of Aircraft and Personnel (TRAP). A mission performed by an assigned and briefed aircrew for the specific purpose of the recovery of personnel, equipment, and/or aircraft when the tactical situation precludes search and rescue assets from responding and when survivors and their location have been confirmed. Also called TRAP.[23]

---

[1] Chairmen Joint Chiefs of Staff, JP 3-02, GL-6.

[2] United States Marine Corps, Marine Corps Reference Publication (MCRP) 5-12C, *Marine Corps Supplement to the Department of Defense Dictionary of Military and Associated Terms* (Washington, DC: Headquarters, United States Marine Corps, 2011), II-2.

[3] United States Marine Corps, Marine Corps Warfighting Publication (MCWP) 3-2, *Aviation Operations* (Washington, DC: Headquarters, United States Marine Corps, 2000), 2-3.

[4] Ibid.

[5] Ibid., 2-4.

[6] United States Marine Corps, MCRP 5-12C, II-3.

[7] Chairmen Joint Chiefs of Staff, JP 3-02, GL-8.

[8] United States Marine Corps, MCRP 5-12C, II-6.

[9] Ibid., II-7.

[10] Ibid., II-8.

[11] United States Marine Corps, MCWP 3-2, 2-4.

[12] Ibid., 2-3.

[13] United States Marine Corps, MCRP 5-12C, II-17.

[14] United States Marine Corps, MCWP 3-2, 2-4.

[15] Chairmen Joint Chiefs of Staff, JP 3-02, XV.

[16] United States Marine Corps, MCRP 5-12C, II-30 to II-40.

[17] Ibid., II-41.

[18] Ibid., II-43.

[19] Chairmen Joint Chiefs of Staff, JP 3-02, GL-14.

[20] United States Marine Corps, MCRP 5-12C, II-47.

[21] Chairmen Joint Chiefs of Staff, JP 3-02, GL-15.

[22] Ibid., GL-16.

[23] United States Marine Corps, MCWP 3-2, 2-3 to 2-4.

COMMANDER'S INTENT AND LETTER TO ALL HANDS

The following documents were provided to the author via an email from General Mattis dated October 2, 2014. They represent his commander's intent from Task Force 58 and 1st Marine Division 2003. Also included is a letter to all hands of 1st Marine Division. All markings are General Mattis's.

# Operation ENDURING FREEDOM – Nov 2001

Purpose: Working in concert with TF SWORD, Amphibious Raid Forces will maintain constant pressure on Talban/Al Qaida forces, creating chaos and destabilizing enemy control of southern Afghanistan.

I intend to exploit the enemy's focus on active ground operations in northern Afghanistan. Coordinating, integrating and deconflicting with TF SWORD, Amphibious Raid Forces will attack the Taliban in southern Afghanistan with repeated raids designed to destroy the enemy's sense of security and shatter his will. Amphibious Raid Forces will exploit TF SWORD's successes and maintain the momentum gained by SWORD, attacking targets that compel the enemy to react, exposing him to our combined arms.

End State:
•Taliban/Al Qaida Leaders in disarray, facing an operational dilemma on how to allocate their forces (northern front or southern Afghanistan).
•Freedom for TF-58 to operate on the ground at the time and place of our choosing.
•Destroy Taliban leadership's confidence that they maintain any control over southern Afghanistan.

MICHAEL – NOT SURE IF YOU HAVE THERE. JUST FYI.

GOING INTO AFG W/ TF 58

# Operation IRAQI FREEDOM – Feb 2003

Commander's Intent: We will swiftly secure key oil nodes allowing the least possible opportunity for their destruction. We will shatter enemy forces south of the Euphrates, west of the Shatt al Basrah and east of An Nasiriyah, opening the MSR and gaining positions north of the river to facilitate operations in the vicinity of Al Kut via Routes 1, 7 or 6 as the situation dictates. In order to achieve tactical surprise we will first blind enemy reconnaissance, then close on the border. We will be prepared to accept enemy capitulation, but destroy the 51st Mech Division and its adjacent/supporting units if they fight. To the greatest extent possible, we will limit enemy or friendly damage to the oil infrastructure.

We must neutralize enemy artillery through shaping, preparatory, or responsive counter fires. I expect maximum use of air fires; assault support will be used if rapid linkup is achievable. Speed is the measure: speed coupled with harmony of information flow; rapidity in decision making; orders promulgation; counter fire; response to changing conditions; resupply; CASEVAC; identification of multiple routes; obstacle reduction; maneuver; relief in place; and hand off of EPWs. We will avoid all possible forward passages of lines and any other mingling of forces, and whenever possible create conditions of chaos for our enemies. Aggressive tempo and initiative are vital. Once we have seized the nodes, we will rapidly hand over the zone and EPWs to 1st UK Div and reposition north of Jalibah. Crossing the Euphrates and moving against Al Kut, 1st MarDiv supports 3ID's attack along our western flank, denying the enemy the opportunity to mass against CFLCC's main effort.

The endstate will place the oil infrastructure safely in 1st UK Division's hands; 51st Mech and associated elements eliminated as a threat to Coalition Ops; our Division oriented against Al Kut; and the enemy's units facing absolute destruction if they choose to fight.

**"No better friend, no worse enemy."**

OIF-1 CG's INTENT –
WHILE I INTENDED TO SEIZE THE
TIGRIS RIVER APPROACHES/CROSSING
POINTS, OUR HHQ ORDER WAS
VERY LIMITED. WE ASSUMED WE
WOULD GO TO B-DAD (AND BEYOND)
MY INITIAL INTENT WAS LIMITED
BY THE GEOGRAPHIC LIMITS IN THE
INCOMPLETE INVASION ORDER.

# 1st Marine Division (REIN)

## *Commanding General's Message to All Hands*

For decades, Saddam Hussein has tortured, imprisoned, raped and murdered the Iraqi people; invaded neighboring countries without provocation; and threatened the world with weapons of mass destruction. The time has come to end his reign of terror. On your young shoulders rest the hopes of mankind.

When I give you the word, together we will cross the Line of Departure, close with those forces that choose to fight, and destroy them. Our fight is not with the Iraqi people, nor is it with members of the Iraqi army who choose to surrender. While we will move swiftly and aggressively against those who resist, we will treat all others with decency, demonstrating chivalry and soldierly compassion for people who have endured a lifetime under Saddam's oppression.

Chemical attack, treachery, and use of the innocent as human shields can be expected, as can other unethical tactics. Take it all in stride. Be the hunter, not the hunted: never allow your unit to be caught with its guard down. Use good judgement and act in best interests of our Nation.

You are part of the world's most feared and trusted force. Engage your brain before you engage your weapon. Share your courage with each other as we enter the uncertain terrain north of the Line of Departure. Keep faith in your comrades on your left and right and Marine Air overhead. Fight with a happy heart and strong spirit.

For the mission's sake, our country's sake, and the sake of the men who carried the Division's colors in past battles-*who fought for life and never lost their nerve*-carry out your mission and *keep your honor clean*. Demonstrate to the world there is "No Better Friend, No Worse Enemy" than a U.S. Marine.

J.N. Mattis
Major General, U.S. Marines
Commanding

# APPENDIX B

## CONSENT AND USE AGREEMENT FOR ORAL HISTORY MATERIALS

CONSENT AND USE AGREEMENT FOR ORAL HISTORY MATERIALS

You have the right to choose whether or not you will participate in this oral history interview, and once you begin you may cease participating at any time without penalty. The anticipated risk to you in participating is negligible and no direct personal benefit has been offered for your participation. If you have questions about this research study, please contact the student at:_mlvalenti@gmail.com_ or Dr. Robert F. Baumann, Director of Graduate Degree Programs, at (913) 684-2742.

To: Director, Graduate Degree Programs
Room 4508, Lewis & Clark Center
U.S. Army Command and General Staff College

1. I, ___James N. Mattis___, participated in an oral history interview conducted by

_Maj Michael L. Valenti, USMC_, a graduate student in the Master of Military Art and Science

28 OCT 14 - MLV

Degree Program, on the following date [s]: __27 Oct 14__ concerning the following topic:

__Commander Task Force 58 and CG 1st MARDIV OIF I__.

2. I understand that the recording [s] and any transcript resulting from this oral history will belong to the U.S. Government to be used in any manner deemed in the best interests of the Command and General Staff College or the U.S. Army, in accordance with guidelines posted by the Director, Graduate Degree Programs and the Center for Military History. I also understand that subject to security classification restrictions I will be provided with a copy of the recording for my professional records. In addition, prior to the publication of any complete edited transcript of this oral history, I will be afforded an opportunity to verify its accuracy.

3. I hereby expressly and voluntarily relinquish all rights and interests in the recording [s] with the following caveat:

__None          Other: _____

I understand that my participation in this oral history interview is voluntary and I may stop participating at any time without explanation or penalty. I understand that the tapes and transcripts resulting from this oral history may be subject to the Freedom of Information Act, and therefore, may be releasable to the public contrary to my wishes. I further understand that, within the limits of the law, the U.S. Army will attempt to honor the restrictions I have requested to be placed on these materials.

| JAMES N. MATTIS | _signature_ | 28 OCT 2014 |
|---|---|---|
| Name of Interviewee | Signature | Date |
| MICHAEL L. VALENTI | _signature_ | 28 OCT 14 |
| Accepted on Behalf of the Army by | | Date |

# BIBLIOGRAPHY

## Primary Sources

Broadmeadow, LtCol John J. "Logistics Support to 1st Marine Division During Operation Iraqi Freedom." *Marine Corps Gazette* 87, no. 8 (August 2003): 44-45.

Commander, Task Force 58. "Operation Enduring Freedom, CTF-58, Narrative Summary, Operations In Afghanistan, 27 October 2001 to 26 February 2002."

_____. "Task Force 58 Command Chronology for the Period 27 October to 26 February 2002." February 21, 2002.

_____. "Thoughts About TF58: Nov 2001-Apr 2002." November 23, 2010.

Kelly, BGen John F. "Tikrit, South to Babylon." *Marine Corps Gazette* 88, no. 2 (February 2004): 16-19.

Lethin, LtCol Clarke R. "1st Marine Division and Operation Iraqi Freedom." *Marine Corps Gazette* 88, no. 2 (February 2004): 20-22.

Mattis, MajGen James N. "The Professional Edge." *Marine Corps Gazette* 88, no. 2 (February 2004): 19-20.

Mattis, LtGen James N. "Commanding General's Command and Control (C2) Intent." *Marine Corps Gazette* 90, no. 8 (August 2006): 16-19.

Slim, Field Marshal Sir William. "Kermit Roosevelt Lecture." Lecture, US Army Command and General Staff College, Fort Leavenworth, KS, April 8, 1952.

## Primary Source Interviews

Mattis, Gen James N. Interview by Capt Crossland, February 24, 2002, interview CDR-699. Transcript, Marine Corps Oral History Program, Marine Corps History and Museum Division, Quantico, VA.

_____. Interview by Dr. Gary Solis, June 18, 2007, interview 0052. Transcript, Marine Corps Oral History Program, Marine Corps History and Museum Division, Quantico, VA.

_____. Interview by Harry Kreisler, March 20, 2014, interview #28135. Conversations with History, University of California at Berkley, Berkley, CA. University of California Television. Accessed August 29, 2014. http://www.uctv.tv/shows/ Reflections-with-General-James-Mattis-Conversations-with-History-28135.

_____. Telephone conversation with author, Lansing, KS, October 28, 2014.

# Books

Braddon, Russell. *The Siege.* New York: The Viking Press, 1969.

Clausewitz, Carl von. *On War.* Translated by Michael Howard, Peter Paret, and Bernard Brodie. Princeton, NJ: Princeton University Press, 1984.

Collins, James C. *Good to Great: Why Some Companies Make the Leap--and Others Don't.* New York: HarperBusiness, 2001.

Coram, Robert. Boyd. *The Fighter Pilot Who Changed the Art of War.* Boston: Little, Brown, 2002.

Gordon, Michael R., and Bernard E. Trainor. *Cobra II: The Inside Story of the Invasion and Occupation of Iraq.* New York: Vintage Books, 2006.

Groen, LtCol Michael S. *With the 1st Marine Division in Iraq, 2003: No Greater Friend, No Worse Enemy.* Quantico: History Division Marine Corps University, 2006.

Klein, Gary A. *Sources of Power: How People Make Decisions.* Cambridge, MA: MIT Press, 1998.

Kuhn, Thomas S. *The Structure of Scientific Revolutions.* 4th ed. Chicago: The University of Chicago Press, 2012.

Lowrey, Nathan S. *U.S. Marines In Afghanistan, 2001-2002: FROM THE SEA: U.S. Marines in the Global War on Terrorism.* Washington, DC: United States Marine Corps History Division, 2011.

McCoy, B. P. *The Passion of Command: The Moral Imperative of Leadership.* Quantico, VA: Marine Corps Association, 2006.

Slim, William Joseph. *Defeat Into Victory.* London: Macmillan, 1986.

Stewart, Richard W., ed. *American Military History: The United States Army in a Global Era, 1917-2008. 2005.* 2nd ed. Vol. 2. Washington, DC: Center of Military History United States Army, 2010.

Sun Tzu. *The Art of War.* Translated by Samuel B. Griffith. London: Oxford University Press, 1971.

## Journal Articles

Goulding, Vincent. "Task Force 58: a Higher Level of Naval Operation." *Marine Corps Gazette* 95, no. 8 (August 2011): 38-41. Accessed March 23, 2014. https://www.mca-marines.org/gazette/2011/08/task-force-58-higher-level-naval-operation.

Kirk, Maj Christopher J. "The Demise of Decision Making: How Information Superiority Degrades Our Ability to Make Decisions." */luce.nt/ A Journal of National Security Studies* (Fall 2014): 84-93. Accessed October 30, 2014. https://www.usnwc.edu/Publications/-Luce-nt-/Current/Pdfs/Kirk_The-Demise-of-Decision-Making-Colbert_Kirk-C-.aspx.

Shillaber, B. P. "Grierson's Raid." *Journal of the United States Cavalry Association* 14, no. 52 (April 1904): 684-710.

Willeford, SgtMaj James D. "What Is a Military Professional?: Do we have a professional enlisted corps?" *Marine Corps Gazette* 98, no. 9 (September 2014): 95-99.

## Doctrinal Publications

Chairman Joint Chiefs of Staff. Joint Publication 3-02, *Amphibious Operations*. Washington, DC: US Government Printing Office, 2014.

Department of the Navy. Naval Tactics Techniques and Procedures 3-02.1M, *Ship-To-Shore Movement*. Newport, RI: Navy Warfare Development Command, 2007.

Headquarters, United States Marine Corps. *Marine Corps Manual w/ CH 1-3*. Washington, DC: United States Marine Corps, 1980.

United States Marine Corps. Marine Corps Doctrinal Publication 1, *Warfighting*. Washington, DC: Headquarters, United States Marine Corps, 1997.

———. Marine Corps Doctrinal Publication 1-0, *Marine Corps Operations*. Washington, DC: Headquarters, United States Marine Corps, 2011.

———. Marine Corps Doctrinal Publication 3, *Expeditionary Operations*. Washington, DC: Headquarters, United States Marine Corps, 1998.

———. Marine Corps Warfighting Publication 3-2, *Aviation Operations*. Washington, DC: Headquarters, United States Marine Corps, 2000.

———. Marine Corps Warfighting Publication 3-24, *Assault Support*. Washington, DC: Headquarters, United States Marine Corps, 2004.

_____. Marine Corps Reference Publication 5-12C, *Marine Corps Supplement to the Department of Defense Dictionary of Military and Associated Terms.* Washington, DC: Headquarters, United States Marine Corps, 2011.

Internet

Headquarters, United States Marine Corps. "Marine Corps 101." October 17, 2013. Accessed June 6, 2014. http://www.hqmc.marines.mil/Portals/61/ MarineCorps101.pdf.

_____. "Official Biography: General James N. Mattis." Accessed November 8, 2014. https://slsp.manpower.usmc.mil/gosa/biographies/rptBiography.asp?PERSON_ID =121&PERSON_TYPE=General.

52029196R00055

Made in the USA
San Bernardino, CA
04 September 2019